THE ANTE-ROOM

THE
ANTE-ROOM

BY

LOVAT DICKSON

LONDON
MACMILLAN & CO LTD
1959

MACMILLAN AND COMPANY LIMITED
London Bombay Calcutta Madras Melbourne

THE MACMILLAN COMPANY OF CANADA LIMITED
Toronto

To the memory of
JACK SQUIRE
Poet, man of letters,
and unforgettable friend

In my first flower-time, when the lily broke its sheath,
Each day brought surprise from the dark lake underneath:
I wondered unknowing when I lay down at night
What image at morning would burn upon my sight.

J. C. SQUIRE

CHAPTER ONE

THE sense of awe with which I had begun the day had turned after many monotonous hours into fretful tiredness. The carriage swam forward on the rough sandy track it had been following ever since we had left the railway that morning. I was four years old, hot and tired, and longing to see my mother who would be waiting for us at our new home at the journey's end. Laura, our nursemaid, sat between my brother and me, and on the opposite seat, facing the way from which we had come, sat Mr. Barclay, the Assay clerk, whose job it had been to meet us in Kalgoorlie.

Mr. Barclay was loquacious and full of information, and I had grown tired of him and his voice. But I knew that Laura — nobody knew Laura as well as I did — was fascinated with him, and was acting silly. To make her aware of this, I had become tiresome, and had been slapped and shaken by Laura in return. Mr. Barclay droned on while I watched this strange, frightening world of undulating sand-plains, mallee scrub and desert gum trees slide by.

Overhead the blue sky was a glaring wall, hard with heat. The trunks of the trees were white with drought, and the scrub growing close to the track we followed was stunted, grey and lifeless. Laura and Mr. Barclay, absorbed in their chatter, did not appear to feel it, but

I

I can remember after all these years the sense of desolation this landscape produced in me. Even the air seemed glassy and unreal. It was as though we followed a track along the bed of a sea. The stunted scrub and the lifeless trees were submarine growths. One looked through the glassy air as through water. I had to struggle to get to the top of my breath each time I breathed. I shivered, and was afraid.

From time to time Mr. Barclay would address himself to me or my brother, to point out something remarkable. A long camel train swinging towards us, returning from the mine to the point on the railway fifty miles away from which we had come. The stench of the camels as they passed made my eyes smart and my stomach rise; the cloud of dust their passage raised billowed through the carriage and we had to wave our hats violently to get rid of it. Mr. Barclay explained to Laura that everything that was brought to Lawlers, every bit of machinery for the mine, as well as nearly all the food, had to be freighted in by camel train. Laura had her big hand to her mouth in fright, seeing the bearded Afghans who rode the camels, and I shot a look at her that was meant to say 'I told you so !'

We had passed, two or three times during that day, groups of aborigines gathered round their cooking-pots in the shade of trees. These were the first blacks I had seen living wild. We knew aborigines in Eastern Australia, but they were respectably in employment or seeking it, they were a part of the familiar background of life. Suddenly here they were living in the scrub, and I responded to Laura's trembling arm around my shoulder, and the sharp intake of her breath, with a shiver. I saw them often in the next few years, and I never

ceased to be afraid of them. I was solemnly warned
by Mr. Barclay never to wander away from home or
I would be stolen ! Seeing them look up from their
smoke-blackened cooking-pots as we passed, smelling
the acrid smell of their bodies, looking into their weak
lashless eyes, I had no need to be warned. These home-
less creatures, who lived out their days wandering over
the face of this dusty scrub-bitten earth, were the constant background of our lives.

All of a sudden our home rose out of this barren
waste. Suddenly there were chimney stacks, and houses,
and dusty streets with shops and hitching-poles outside,
and horses standing wilting in the heat, and men waving
straw hats at us. Suddenly in an isolated place was
home, after all these weeks of travel, with my mother
in a white dress appearing on the verandah. We had
come together again. The agony of the child who fears
he may be forgotten along the way was over. It was
bliss to hear the sounds and smell the familiar smells
associated with home, the mill stamps' thundering crash,
the odour of my father's cigar, my mother's happy
laughter, the deep murmur of my father's voice.

We seemed in those days always to be on the move.
My father was never with us on these journeys. He
had always gone on ahead, and we were perpetually
rushing to catch up with him. He was making his
career. He was a man who moved fast, but my mother
was his match, and she managed with the help of Tom,
our black groom, whom my mother's brother, Uncle
Bill, had brought back from the Boer War, and with
Laura and the enormous paraphernalia of a family
travelling, to keep up. In the early morning light
of childhood, it was fierce and exciting, as well as

worrying, this constant movement and bustle and rush.
New horizons were continually unfolding before our
eyes ; we were loved by our parents, who were then
still immersed in their own love for each other, and
who played with us as with toys.

We were a Colonial family, and were proud of it.
We passionately believed in the British Empire, and
especially in England. I do not think my own family
was more fanatical or peculiar in this regard than the
others we had known and had intermarried with in the
two hundred years since we had left the misty islands,
good Presbyterians that we were, driven out by the
sword that would have made us bow our stiff necks at
Communion, and say Amen to prayers composed by
bishops in London. We were of that race called
Scotch-Irish, who had gone in Covenanting times from
Midlothian and Ayrshire and neighbouring parts of
Scotland to Ireland, had stayed there for a generation,
and then gone across the seas to America, taking with
us our Bibles and our households and our unbending
rectitude, and because we were romantic Scots by
nature and Presbyterians only by persuasion, taking
with us also the precious memory of the 'lone shieling
of the misty island', and keeping it enshrined in our
minds for evermore.

This explained us, and made reasonable what would
otherwise appear to be an excess of eccentricity. My
great-grandfather William, for example, who had become by the standards of his time wealthy as a ship-
owner, made a voyage round the world in one of his

own ships, and slept every night under the British flag. When the ship was in a foreign port he slept on board, and it gave him great pride afterwards to count the many nights he had slept comfortably on solid, ordered earth where Britain held sway.

We had been taught generation after generation to think and speak of England with respect and veneration. Long before I saw it I had an image of England in my mind, the way in church behind your closed eyes you see the altar and the cross standing at its centre. We were a little ostentatious in the display of our feelings which ran deep, and in a hundred ways obeisance was made to the image we carried in our daily life. I am thinking here not only of my own family but of countless others like us who made up the solid, steady, sober, industrious people, the majority of them of Scottish origin, who had, with that blend of dour endurance and blind obstinacy which can when needed become iron determination, of sheer romanticism which on occasion can inspire the daring deed that can turn defeat into victory, really built the British Empire. It had its snobbish, and sometimes its silly side. Perhaps the family crests we blazoned on our carriages, stamped on our notepaper and wore on our signet rings, might have been challenged at the College of Arms. But perhaps they might not. No records could have been kept more meticulously than those written up in the back of great family Bibles, and passed from one generation to another. My strongest earliest memories are of standing often beside my grandmother who had the Bible open upon her knee while she told me stories of our past. She was a lady of some account in her own right. She had been a direct descendant of the

Lovats of Beauly and had been spending a winter with her parents at Hobart, staying with her cousin, Sir Peter Gordon, when she met my grandfather and married him. Her own considerable family history was, however, submerged in the broader family legend, the exploits and achievements of the gentlemen farmers who drove the French out of Acadia, and won Canada for the Empire, that being considered, perhaps rightly, of greater account than what my grandmother's Frasers had done.

We had in fact, far back in the family's history, displayed some heroism for England's sake, but had been amply rewarded for it. As a family our roots were deeply in Canada, going back through generation after generation of large spilling families to the year 1756, when the French hinge on the North American continent was broken by the capture of Nova Scotia, and the way was laid open for the final settlement with the French three years later on the Plains of Abraham at Quebec. The force of New England volunteers who, with a few regular troops, had triumphed in this operation, had succeeded in breaking the hinge by which the French maintained a constant pressure against the Anglo-Saxon communities strung out along the Atlantic seaboard, 'encroaching on our backsides' as my sturdy ancestors were always complaining to London.

Relieved to have got the French army out of Nova Scotia, these gentlemen farmers from New England, under the wise leadership of Governor Shirley of Massachusetts, were not for taking chances with the loyalty of the inhabitants. Anticipating Hitler and Stalin, they set on foot the first great expulsion of modern times, removing the Acadian inhabitants to points more than a thousand miles from their former homes, and turning over to individuals who had played a part in this important conquest the rich land of which these French farmers had been dispossessed. Of this event the poet Longfellow made much in 'Evangeline', the story of a young girl separated from her lover in this vast act of dispossession. There is no question that it was a harsh measure, but Longfellow over-sentimentalized his tale, and peace came as a result instead of continuing war.

Among the prominent beneficiaries of this large-scale hand-out was the uncle of my great-great-grandfather, Major Charles Dickson, a retired army officer who had led the exodus from Ireland, and had settled in Connecticut some years before. He had raised a company which played a leading part in the expedition to capture Acadia. For his share in the enterprise he was given three thousand acres of the richest land in the Minas Basin. He had no children. His heir was his brother's child, my great-great-grandfather, also named Charles. He had come to the province in 1760, as a boy of sixteen, and with his marriage and the birth of his large family we became Canadians.

Later, when I was old enough, and as a boy of fifteen found myself on my own in Canada, I could comprehend something of what these New England families felt for this land, beautiful and seductive even in those alarming times when the Indians were outside every stockade, and privateers could emerge from the sea-fog at any moment, to make a sudden raid upon the land. Here in this crisp cold Northern air, on acres washed by these green seas with their great sweeping tides, there would have been a sense of vigour, of promise for the future, not felt so keenly in the older settlements they had left along the Connecticut shore. My great-great-grandfather Charles was ambitious and hard-working, and he was lucky. From the sea's edge in Nova Scotia the land went back thick with timber. He farmed his uncle's acres, he became a large-scale fisherman, selling his cod caught on the Grand Banks as far away as Europe; and with the timber they cleared, he and all his neighbours built ships badly needed in the war against Napoleon. In the next generation, before the coming of iron ships, the wooden Nova Scotian schooners, known as Bluenoses, penetrated the harbours of the world. There was a peak time when one out of every four ships that 'went foreign' were Bluenose schooners with their home ports in Nova Scotia; not in Halifax only, but in the creeks and tidal waterways that ran in a hundred different places back into the folds of the land, where big families with their domestic servants and workmen lived in little communities, families intermarrying with families until everyone was 'cousin' to everyone else.

Charles had ten children, of whom my great-grand-father William was the fourth of four sons. All the sons married, as did all the daughters except one. One son, Charles, married Rachel Archibald; two girls, Olivia and Elizabeth, married Archibald boys. The Archibalds were another family like ours who had come to Nova Scotia twenty-three years before the great rush of United Empire Loyalists poured in after the Revolution. My great-grandfather William and two of his brothers and two of his Archibald brothers-in-law were members of the Nova Scotia Legislative

Assembly. Since there were then less than fifty members altogether, it can be seen how the affairs of this Colony were managed by a close tissue of inter-related families.

Charles died in 1796 of Yellow Fever caught on a voyage on one of his ships home from the Barbados. My great-great-grandmother, having news in Truro that he had been landed from his ship in Halifax in a dying state, made the seventy-mile journey across country on horseback in two days to be at his deathbed. Pioneer women were like that, tireless, loyal and loving, capable of such physical endurance even at middle age.

He survived only a few days after she reached Halifax. Instantly, from the position of authority in the home, although she was only forty-two, she stepped down, giving up the place to John's wife, for he was the eldest son. But she was by no means out of life's race. With such a large family there was always some crisis to engage her interest: the birth of grandchildren, the engagements, the weddings, even an abduction.

Samuel George William Archibald, a young advo-cate, who was to become a famous son of Nova Scotia, had an 'understanding' with one of her daughters, Mary. A younger sister, Elizabeth, the beauty of the family, was at the age of sixteen, in 1802, at school at a 'select academy for young ladies' at Wolfville. Young Archibald, having occasion to go to Wolfville to plead a cause, carried a gift from her mother to Elizabeth. Arriving at the school, he found her in disgrace for some offence, and confined to her room on bread and water. Tearfully she begged him to help her escape from this horrid place, and the clever young lawyer lost his head and his heart at the same time. Forgetting his case, and evidently ignoring the consequences of what he was about to do, he got Elizabeth on an excuse to the front door where his horse was tied, to see him off, mounted, seized her and lifted her up behind him, and rode away from the school. They were married a week afterwards.

But I think of the shock of death in these households, especially the effect on them of the death of the head of the family like Charles. How much it changed the situation of them all, from the widow like Amelia, who must now take second place, down to the negro slaves disposed of under the Will on these occasions : 'I give and bequeath my negro woman to my beloved wife during her lifetime, and after her death at her disposal : I give and bequeath my negro boy called Prince to my son Stephen during his lifetime and after that to his surviving son'. . . . One sees, as so often in the past in the disposal of property on these momentous occasions, a reflection of how they lived, of the unchanging pattern of their lives, taken over from the generation before them, and passed on to the generation following, even to the negro slaves they had brought with them from the American Colonies forty years before, who under British rule were actually liberated. But this point was finely ignored by those who disposed of them testamentarily, and even sometimes by the 'property' themselves who often obstinately refused to go free. In the recorded words of one of them, 'Master, you eated me when I wuz meat, now you must pick me when I'se bone.'

My great-grandfather William, born in 1779, was a youth of seventeen when his father died, and his mother made her ride across country on horseback. With his three elder brothers he carried on the shipbuilding

business and like his father became a member of the
Legislative Assembly. He married Rebecca Pearson,
the daughter of an old New England family, which had
been settled as long in the province as his had, and they
produced a large family of thirteen children, of whom
my grandfather Henry, born in 1824, was the youngest
but one.

When my great-grandfather William died in 1834,
Henry Dickson was a boy of only ten. For some
years after my great-great-grandfather's death the
family shipbuilding business had been carried on by
William and his brothers, but it appears to have lost a
lot of money and finally it was dissolved, even though
Canada had by then not reached the peak of its ship-
owning fortunes. But while you could dispose of an
unprofitable shipyard you could not, even if you had
wanted to, dispose of a universal interest in the making
of ships, the sailing of ships and the carrying of cargo,
and this must have been constant in my grandfather's
young life. In nearly every one of the indented bays of
Nova Scotia, the community was engaged in building
ships or sailing the ships they had built. Even what
they grew on land they carried as freight to sea. The
owners of the ships were generally families like ours
or the Archibalds, the de Wolfes and the Allisons, who
had come to the province and remained the leaders of
the neighbourhood, and the crews were the husbands,
fathers, sons and brothers of the place. Each man
would know his ship from her keel upwards, from her
ribs inwards, for he had helped to build her. He
would even have helped to make with his own hands
her suits of sails. The storms they weathered crossing
the Atlantic or going round the Horn, the curious things

and tales they gathered on long voyages to India or Africa,
the record runs they had made, the wealth they brought
home : all this was bred into the bone of Nova Scotia
boys, and there was no question as to what was to be
done with the two boys not yet started in life when my
great-grandfather died, Horatio, my grandfather's elder
brother (always called Rache in our family), and my
grandfather, Henry. Having finished school at Pictou
Academy as all their brothers and their uncles in the
previous generation had done, they would go into shipping. Both boys were taken into the de Wolfe family
business with which they had a connection through
their uncle Robert.

Thus began my grandfather Henry's long connection
with the sea which was to last, with all its varying
fortunes, to his death. He began by sailing round the
Horn in a de Wolfe ship. He would have heard of this
run all his life ; it was a testing place for ships and men,
the roaring Forties, which seamen called 'Old Stiff',
where the gales have a clear sweep from the Antarctic
and the enormous grey-backed Cape Horners are the
biggest seas in the world.

He survived it coming and going to San Francisco
in 1851, and as happens with people who love the sea,
the more it frightened him the more he loved it. He
had sailed before on a deep-waterman, to Maine and
Connecticut and the Yankee ports, and once to England
with his uncle. But on these occasions he had been
small and was classed as a passenger. Now he was
called upon, with his little store of knowledge and his
slender strength, to be an apprentice on a voyage that
would last several months.

He never forgot that first voyage. Who would

have done! From the evening tide on which they left Halifax harbour, and the outlines of home faded in the summer sky, until he returned on a windy morning in October, the voyage took four months. They rounded the Horn in classically stormy weather. A hurricane raged from the Antarctic; the seas were wild and boiling, so tumultuous that the truck of a tall passing ship, staggering along to leeward, could not be seen except when both ships were topping the crest. This was no series of huge waves fast upon one another's heels, threatening to drown the clipper, but a spilling earthquake of grey, boiling water with separate volcanoes hissing and spuming and vast craters suddenly opening in the thudding depths. A wooden ship is like a living thing, and in such a storm she groaned and whimpered in every part. The following seas ran on, each one threatening to overwhelm the ship as with a shuddering pause it held her motionless before cascading its tons of water on the deck.

There was no doubt about it, you had to be born to the sea to stand it; you had to feel yourself at such a moment as much a part of the ship as the hull which was withstanding this tremendous battering, and terrified though you were, your heart in your mouth as it must be after every shock of a breaking mother-wave, when a ship lies utterly helpless for a minute, her deck awash with foaming water, her crew clinging to the rigging and the stays; you had to feel even at these moments a quick flicker of defiance. With the wind howling and moaning in the rigging, and the spindrift blown from the tossing crests into your stiff face, you had to feel a little jagged sense of triumph streak through you each time the ship righted herself and

B

hurled herself again at the roaring walls of water.

Henry never forgot that first voyage, neither the storms nor the other days when the ship rode with the wind, rising exultantly to meet each fresh wave as a steeplechaser leaps at a fence, with the men on deck busy under the direction of the mate, singing in their deep male voices the shanties he had heard as a boy in the parlours of Pictou, at evening time under the lamplight, when you could see the faces of women sewing, and smell the sweet smell of home, while someone thundered out:

> What ho, Piper ! watch her how she goes !
> Give her sheet and let her rip.
> We're the boys to pull her through.
> You ought to see her rolling home ;
> For she's the gal to go
> In the passage home in ninety days
> From Cal-i-for-ni-o.

Someone who knew my grandfather at that time wrote : 'His appearance is striking, being tall and well-built, with blue eyes, dark hair and handsome features. Although inclined to be of a somewhat choleric temper he has the most courtly manners and speech, with a wealth of expression in both talking and writing.' He was eighteen years old at this time, and at the beginning of a period of adventure and travel which was to last over the next seven years, through South America, India, Africa and Australia. In 1851 he returned to the de Wolfe office in Liverpool, and later in London, until in 1853 he formed a company of his own, named Dickson, Williams & Company, and in 1857 opened an office in Melbourne as agent for the principal shipping lines of the day including Money, Wigram & Company, The Blackwall Line and Josiah Heap & Company of Liverpool. He married my grandmother in 1862 and built Ticarra in Balaclava, a growing and fashionable suburb of Melbourne at that time. Today, where once the house stood, with its wide verandah and balconies and the steep sweep of garden, where the horses which my father remembered as a small boy galloped in the paddocks or stood in the heat of the day, switching their tails under the great wattle trees, there is only a featureless waste of bricks and mortar. Where once the ground was thick with flowers and the scent of the rich earth was pungent in the nostrils, there is now only the sharp smell of a modern city. Even in Australia, time like a river rolls on, leaving its residual deposit in the twentieth century of concrete and paving-stone and chimney-stack pricking at the sky.

I am not going to write about my vigorous ancestors but about myself in the pages that follow. But I could not explain my own character without calling them briefly to appear. What they did, what they endured, their achievements, their failures, their tempers and ardours, the workings of their minds and the inclination of their hearts moulded me into what I am. They are accessories before the fact, just as in my conduct of my life I make a pattern for those who will follow me.

My father, after an early and unsuccessful start in my grandfather's shipping offices in London and Australia,

had gone to the School of Mines and had become a
Mining Engineer. By the time we children were born
he had established a reputation as a successful manager
of mining properties. We followed wherever he went:
my mother, the four children, Laura, and Dick, the
white groom who had succeeded Tom, the black one.
We travelled by train, by ship, by stage-coach; sometimes by horse and buggy, and once, a journey of several
days, by bullock team in Rhodesia.

My parents had not been able to marry without
a great deal of opposition from my grandparents on
my father's side, who were proud with that pride
that now seems old-fashioned, but which was characteristic of so many families of our kind in mid-Victorian
times, especially amongst those who lived in far-off
parts of the British world. My Dickson grandparents
thought that my mother's family, the Cunninghams,
were not good enough for their son. And the Cunninghams, a Catholic family, mounted and vociferated their
opposition, too. This was based not only on my
father's religious faith, but on the intolerable fact that
if Jo married Gordon she would be taken away from
them to the other side of the world.

Within three years of his arrival in Australia, my
father had been involved in a railway accident which
almost cost him his life. His left eye was badly damaged
by broken glass, and was always thereafter askew, but I
did not notice this until somebody pointed it out to me
when I was much older. He was sent to recuperate at a
station in the Riverina which was near the station owned
by the Cunninghams. He met my mother at a dance,
and fell in love with her, which automatically meant
falling foul of her seven brothers. These were formidable

young men, renowned in the district for useless feats of strength, like jumping over a stock fence with a live sheep under one arm, or lifting a wagon-load of flour on their backs; renowned also for a boisterous behaviour which had got them into trouble on several occasions.

My mother had been brought up on the Cunningham station, only leaving it to attend a Catholic convent at Mitta-Mitta for her education. She had not met many men when upon the scene came my father, aged twenty-three, fair-haired, thin as a blade, with a very straight and attractive figure; and the sort of voice which evoked scorn, the voice of a 'pommy' who had been educated in England. He had a dark buff overcoat, pleated at the back, with three ridiculous and superfluous buttons just above the vent, and he wore a felt hat.

Up-country in Australia he must have seemed fair game; his 'pommy' accent, his thin hauteur of a kind which is never well-received in pioneer surroundings, as these were in those days; his fragile air, his immense dedication to reading, and his English clothes were also a matter of general offence. But what really aroused the Cunningham brothers to noisy anger was his total disregard of them.

Much of this I heard from my Cunningham uncles afterwards, and a little I remember my mother telling me. The brothers were furious. Everybody rode a horse in those days, and my mother rode to perfection. My father was in the saddle all day, and sometimes half the night. But he came to local dances. He danced with my mother, oblivious of her brothers' displeasure, and he called on her next day, which was Sunday, and took her riding; and it was she who now told her brothers that she needed no escort, and went off into the hills with the thin young man with the damaged eye and the 'pommy' manners, who had taken her fancy and was never to let it go.

I can't pretend to know the details of that courtship of so long ago. I know that they were passionately in love, and that is a good thing. First my sister Mitta was born, named after the Mitta-Mitta River on which at that time my father, who had meanwhile graduated from the School of Mines, was working a prosperous gold claim with Everard and Gerald Browne, the sons of T. A. Browne who, under the pen-name of Rolf Boldrewood, had written a great Australian classic, *Robbery Under Arms*. Next came my sister Irene. Then I appeared, the first son, and two years after me came Clive. We were born as the old century turned into the new, Mitta in 1899, Clive in 1904.

My father had been brought up a strict Protestant, and even in the newness of happy married life he could not abandon the routine so heavily engraved on his life, nor consider my mother's different faith and upbringing. We had morning prayers in the dining-room every day before breakfast; we had a Japanese cook, Keno, who was absolved from attendance, but no one else escaped, even to Laura and Dick the groom. In North-West Australia it was often very hot; all the windows would be open to what little breeze there was; the rhythmic thump of the mill stamps would sound in our ears, as in this waste of scrub and sand we knelt on a turkey-red carpet and listened while my father said the prayers. He was then General

Manager of the Bewick-Moreing mining properties, known as the Northern Mines. Herbert Hoover, who was later to become President of the United States, was a director, and so was Gerald Browne. I can remember them both filling my mind with greater wonder than God, whom we could not see, as they knelt and joined my father in prayer. Herbert Hoover was very stout and he wore a stiff white collar even in this northern desert. The heat wilted it, sweat burst from him as from a thousand springs, but on his broad knees he was made to kneel while appetizing whiffs of the breakfast Keno was preparing came through the screen door.

A church had been built in Lawlers where we lived, but it was of corrugated iron and it offended my father aesthetically. We were a hundred and eighty miles north of Kalgoorlie where, except for a small branch line, the railroad then ended. Low-grade ore could not be milled economically, so he decided to use rock which had gold in it to build an altar that would relieve the church of some of its ugliness. In due course the altar was made and consecrated, and beautiful it was at the east end of the church where the sun struck it during morning services, lighting up in the igneous rock the yellow bloom of gold. But I remember the church best at evening services, when the paraffin lamps were lit and the roof was hot still from the setting sun, and I was tired with the weight of five years; and heard my father's and mother's sweet voices singing, and smelt the scent my mother always used, and was allowed to lean against her breast during the lessons and sermons, and could fall asleep to the mingled scent of paraffin lamp and Parma violets, in that lovely half-light so free of ogres and frights, especially so with my father's long legs touching my thigh, and my mother's breast a soft pillow to my head.

The house in which we lived had, like the rest of the houses in town, only recently been put up, but no expense had been spared to make a young manager in this remote spot content with his lot. The house was of wood, and no tree that grew straight or was worthy of the name was to be found less than hundreds of miles away. The timber could be shipped quite easily to the end of the railway, but beyond that it could not be driven, as we had been, from well to well in the desert. It had to be taken by camel train, mile after mile through the waste of scrub until it reached the point where the mine stood. That was the way our house had come to Lawlers.

It was very comfortable; it was not makeshift. It was large, to begin with, and surrounded on all sides by a deep wide-screened verandah, on which we all slept in beds the legs of which stood in pots of water, to keep out the ants. There was a large drawing-room and dining-room, and to each of us a bedroom, used for keeping clothes in and being private. The sandy wastes fell away on each side, but my father and mother quickly decided on a garden, and I can remember the day when the turf which had been brought all the way from Leonora was laid, and the hoses, fed from the artesian well, started to sprinkle it; and the unaccustomed combination of startling green and sprinkling water held us all spellbound, and in the dusk after we had been sent to bed the exciting sound kept us all awake.

When we left Perth my sisters had come northward with my mother up the coast to Geraldton where they were left in a convent, where I was ultimately to join them for a miserable term.

I loved my father passionately, and with my sisters away at school, Clive and I basked in his full attention. We used to see him only at morning prayers and meal-times, except for an hour at night just before we went to bed when, with a whisky-and-soda in his hand, he would wander about our rooms, or into our bathroom, and talk in an offhand, teasing, delightful way with us. He loved his books, and listening to him read aloud to us, made me love them too. He sent to Perth once for children's books for us; it must have been Christmas-time or on one of our birthdays. But he gave them to us with a scornful remark about the kind of thing that was written for children. He told me once when I was very young: 'You and I like the same things, why shouldn't we like the same books? I won't tell you stories at bedtime, or read to you that trash written for simple hungry minds. But if you would like me to read to you the books I am reading myself, I'll do it with pleasure.' So, night after night during my early childhood, I can remember my father reading to us. Dickens and Thackeray were his great favourites, and naturally became mine. By the time I was eleven and came to England, I had read or had had read to me every novel that Dickens and Thackeray had written, but I did not know more than a dozen children's books; and I did not read until I was out in the world on my own the classics of English literature written for child-hood, *The Water Babies*, the *Alice* books, *The Wind in the Willows*, *Puck of Pook's Hill* and the rest. Instead I read what my father loved and had with him in this barren place : as well as the works of Charles Dickens and Thackeray, some of the novels of Trollope, Australian classics like *Robbery Under Arms*, and Marcus Clarke's *For the Term of His Natural Life*; the stories of Judge Haliburton about Sam Slick, an inheritance from our old family home in Nova Scotia; and of course the poets. It was the age of recitation, when amateurs flourished and entertainment was provided in the home. No one felt self-conscious, neither the audience nor the performers. 'Shelley's "Ode to the West Wind",' someone would say, clearing his throat and striking an appropriate attitude. I was the beneficiary of these performances, for they were often rehearsed before me, for practice, not for my judgment; and I began, even at the age of five, to get an ear for the rhythm and music of great English poetry.

But our minds were not always on these high things. There were moments of extravagant exuberance, too. My father had a horseless carriage shipped to him. It looked exactly like a carriage, and it was beautiful in its new coat of varnish, only it struck us all with wonder because it had no shafts — we sat where the groom usually sat, and beneath the seat was an engine of ex-cessive delicacy but capable of immense vibration and displays of temperament. We were devoured by curi-osity about it in private, but showed impassive faces before the world, leaving it to the miners of Lawlers to be struck dumb with wonderment as on a single cylinder we exploded pop by pop past them; leaving it to them, too, to derive from its frequent breakdowns a ribald mirth. It was kept in the stable which in fact was the only place where cover could be provided for it. But it was like keeping a fox in a hen-house. Long after the last splutter had died away — and how quickly it died away, generally before the machine had reached the courtyard of the stable — the stench of its explosive life hung upon the air, frightening the horses, and according to Dick, taking all the gloss out of their coats.

Fortunately there were mechanics employed by the mine for other purposes, but always at hand to repair the machine, and always curious to conduct an autopsy on it. But often even they were baffled, and for what seemed long periods it would be unusable; and at such times Dick and the horses would come into their own again. Then my father would say that nothing would ever replace the horse. Even as late as the 1930s in Canada, when horses had for all that we counted practical reasons ceased to be, he kept his stable. He loved horses, and was a wonderful horseman, with a hand as delicate and a will to obedience as clear as a horse could wish for.

My mother rode side-saddle. When I rode a pony beside her at the age of five, I can remember thinking how pretty she looked, and being jealous of anyone who talked to her. Dick, the groom, was very proud of her. What had brought Dick to this remote mining town, I do not know. He did not come with my father, who must have been the only man in that part of Australia who had a stable of horses and required a skilled groom. Dick had defects as well as qualities. He was given to oaths and blasphemy, which he tried to restrain himself from using in polite company, but he was powerless sometimes in the face of provocation. I see him now, yellow-skinned, hook-nosed, slack-mouthed, his beady eyes beneath his cap as restless as mechanical toys on sticks, an oath often escaping from his loose lips, like an excess of food that can't be contained in an over-full mouth.

Once I was alone with my mother in the carriage with Dick, driving back from the town of Lawlers, three miles away from the mine. Dick had put in the shafts a particularly mettlesome pair of young horses which my father and he were in the process of breaking in. My mother asked to be allowed to take the reins and Dick refused on the grounds that the pair were too unreliable. My mother insisted, and Dick, to soften his refusal, spread it with oaths as a man spreads his bread with butter. 'You're intolerable, Dick,' my mother cried; 'give me those reins.'

Dick, struggling with the horses which were all over the place, said he would not, but could not say it simply but must hang his refusal with oaths.

'Stop the horses, get down and walk home if you are afraid. Also get down if you cannot speak without swearing. In any event, give me those reins this moment, Dick, or I'll see you are sacked as soon as we get home.'

Dick was mercifully bereft of speech, but I can remember to this moment that he had to stand up, holding on to the reins like a charioteer, while my mother moved over my trembling body to take his place. He had to pass the reins to her and then in turn step across my body to reach her place. Meanwhile we were galloping at the rate of thirty miles an hour and the carriage with no weight in the rear, for we were all on the coachman's seat, was swinging from side to side in the sandy track and threatening at every moment to capsize. Thoroughly frightened, and uneasy lest neither Dick nor my mother should be aware of the danger, I started to howl.

My mother was by now trying to master the horses, and Dick was loudly affirming his dissociation with the wickedness going on about him. But when we came to where the road continued on to the mine but a left turn brought us to the wide clearing before our house, Dick said, 'Keep them running,' and added nothing more, except that his lips continued to mould and fashion what must have been swear-words of the utmost vindictiveness. We approached the house at a gallop, sending up an enormous cloud of dust. My mother said, 'Hold on to me, Rache,' and Dick said again, 'Keep them running. Keep them headed away from the stables.' We passed the house and the hitching-rail outside it in a storm of dust and screaming wheels. We passed the stables a hundred yards farther on in the periphery of a circle. We completed the circumference, and then started to cover it again, still at this blind gallop, still with screaming axles, the thud of hooves on the hard sand, the billowing clouds of dust. And now to the general excitement were added the neighs and screams of horses in the stables, conscious by telepathy that some drama affecting their kind was going on out-side. And now, too, my father came running to the gate. We swept by him on two wheels, covering him with dust, and I had a glimpse of his horrified face, but no more than a glimpse, because by then we had our backs to him and were headed out round the circle.

There was nothing to be done but to let the horses tire. I am sure that it never occurred to my mother to pass the reins back to Dick, and he made no attempt to take them from her. I do not know how many more rounds we made before the horses slackened, and could

be brought sweating to a stop. I had ceased to cry, and
was ready to think now the danger was over that it had
all been rather exciting and splendid. I was ready to be
the centre of attention, marked as having miraculously
survived a hazardous experience. But my mother,
without a word to my father or Dick, ran to her room;
and Dick, without apology or explanation to my
father, mounted the box again and trotted the horses
back to the stables.

I began to chatter about my experience, and was
promptly commanded to silence by my father, herding
me back to the house between the new lawns. 'Oh,
do dry up, old chap, if you don't mind. We've had
quite enough of this subject.' Bereft, forlorn, mis-
understood, I crept along the verandah to the window
which gave on to my mother's bedroom — peered in
at her, thinking that here at least I would be understood;
only to see her lying face downwards on her bed. I
had never seen her weeping before.

There came a day, the most dreadful in my experience, when I was torn from my family and sent among
strangers. Whether it was that I was becoming spoilt,
or the heat in North-Western Australia was approaching
its most intolerable, I don't know. But whatever the
reason, I was condemned to go and join Mitta and Rene
in the convent boarding-school they attended in
Geraldton.

I went with them on their return from a holiday,
and fool that I was, I accepted everyone's assurance that
I was a lucky chap and was going to have the most

wonderful time. I positively looked forward to the moment when I could throw off home ties and step into this brilliant strange world that lay at the end of an exciting journey.

Exciting it was. We rose at five o'clock while it was still dark, when a cool wind blew from the desert, and the stars, strangers to me, who slept when darkness came, were brilliant and beautiful like lamps carried swinging at the knees of an invisible host.

We were to drive the first stage of our journey before the sun rose too high. We breakfasted by lamp-light, and I was burning with excitement. My mother looked at me mournfully and I felt a sudden rush of sympathy for the jealousy she must be feeling at the joy which lay exclusively before me.

When we got into the carriage, Keno was standing at the wheel. He had saved until this actual moment of departure gifts he had for us all, silk kimonos for my sisters, a ceremonial sword for myself, and little boxes of sweets he had made for us. He kissed my hand and laid it against his cheek, and I was a little ashamed of the tenderness he was exhibiting in case it might persuade anyone in authority that I was after all perhaps too young to go. I was not at ease until the rein was slipped from the hitching-rail, the rubber wheels squeaked in the dry sand, and the horses with an exciting twitch of their tails bent their knees to trot off into the darkness. Willing them to go, I could hardly turn back to wave to my parents and Keno, who stood with a weeping Laura behind my mother, forlorn and bereft under the stars.

I do not remember how long it took to get to Geraldton which lay on the Indian Ocean about two hundred miles west of Lawlers. The last part of the journey was made by rail, but the stages we followed with horses must have occupied a full day or even more. Long before we came to the end of that first day I wished myself back home. I had not reckoned with what it meant to be deprived not only of my mother's company, but of Laura's; the livelong day I had had them at my beck and call; now I had only my sisters, stiff and unyielding, and dedicated to the responsibility to which they had been sworn by my mother, of looking after me.

Worse was to befall. This was a girls' school and I was the only boy. The girls were my sisters' age and up to eighteen; I was an insignificant five. It was necessary to keep me apart from them, and I was therefore placed in a whitewashed cell of my own in the nuns' quarters, while my sisters slept in their dormitories. I know now that the nuns meant all their attentions kindly, but isolation had been the extreme punishment at home and they kept me isolated. The interest they showed in me was such a poor substitute for my mother's love that it only served to accentuate my loneliness and loss. And when it came to bath-time, that most happy hour in my life at home, the hollow mockery of what I had known and counted on all my days was so complete that I burst into tears and would not be comforted, nor could I be persuaded that there was nothing to cry about by assurance on that point from the formidable Mother Superior who swept in to see me and to say good-night. Finally one of my sisters was allowed to come and sleep with me. It was Rene — and she was angry with me for the shame I had brought on her, and the loss of the fun in her dormitory of which I had deprived her. It was bliss to be berated by her who was familiar, to feel her warm body against mine, to hear her fierce voice saying what a little fool I was, to feel the sweet breath of home blowing fury into my ear. I slept.

But this could not happen every night, and they tried to train me the way you train a dog, a little kindness mixed with a good deal of firmness, in an attempt to impose their wills on mine. Rene was not allowed to come the second night, and I sobbed myself to sleep. Rene failing me, I tried slyly to find the nun most sympathetic to me in order to win her to be my slave. I can remember her face well, no surprising feat of memory considering the event which engraved it on my mind.

She was young, and in her face, especially in her lips and eyes, I saw with the calculating power of a sharp child the signs of human sympathy, like an ember amongst ashes, which I thought I might fan into something that would help me. Though I have forgotten her name, I can remember that she had large grey eyes and full, very pretty, lips. My shrewd eyes fixed on these, and I played all the cunning tricks I knew to win them to love me.

After tea she had taken me by the hand to the garden, and had shown me the flowers growing there, giving them names which I had never heard before, and telling me little legends of some of them. I loved a story, and these lit my mind.

When we came in she told me to get undressed, put on my shift and come to the bathroom. She would go ahead and run the water in. I got undressed, pulled on the shift which reached to my knees and itched me, and then ran to the bathroom, eager for my friend.

C

It must have been instinctive with her: she had a
pretty way of playing at bath-time, and I allowed myself
little chuckles of mirth as we tackled the games sacred to
this hour. I did not see the ridiculousness of my sitting
in the water in a brown holland shift while such tender
gestures were exchanged between us. After a little
while, carried away by excitement, I pulled up my shift
exhibiting my nakedness and laughed uproariously at
the splendid humour of the thing. Laura would have
responded with a laugh as free, or if she were thinking
of something else, a smart smack on the bottom and an
injunction to get on with my washing. But not like
this, never like this. Tenderness vanished and rigidity
took its place. As stiff as an automaton, I obeyed her
commands. When all of me was washed except my
middle, I was left alone standing in the bath, and did
what the Sister told me to do before she left the
room, pulling up the shift and washing myself, and
then tiptoeing sadly to bed.

I am sure that my parents never guessed the un-
happiness I experienced during those few months in
Geraldton. I never told them, my sisters didn't; and I
suppose that the nuns, patient in this as in all things,
endured the trial I put upon them without complaint.

One day I played football with my straw hat. I
think it blew off my head in a high wind which had
the same effect on my spirits as it had had on my hat.
Sent to chase it, I could not resist giving it a splendid
kick to hoist it still higher in the air. My foot went
through the crown — there it was, impaled on my boot.

We were walking in a crocodile through the streets of Geraldton, the girls two-by-two in front of us, a Sister and I bringing up the rear. The crocodile had stopped for me to rescue my hat, and now I had to remove it from my boot in front of them all. There were no titters. The whole school was deeply ashamed of me, as if in this escapade I had only confirmed its opinion of me as a young barbarian. The crown of my hat remained fastened to the rest only by an inch and because of the boisterous wind, unless I held it on flat with my hand it would flap up and down. This was more than I could bear in the way of indignity, so I tore it off and ground it savagely under my foot. I then took off the brim which alone remained and would have sent that after the rest had not the Sister stopped me. She made me place this remnant back on my head and wear it for the rest of the walk, and the Mother Superior, when she had had a report of my conduct, decreed that I should continue to wear it thus for a week as a punishment.

This, and the other simple miseries I suffered, left me with a dislike of school and authority which remained with me all the rest of my childhood, and which I now discover is still there. And when I returned with my sisters to Lawlers at the end of that term no one, I noticed, asked me if I had enjoyed myself, or if I had had the splendid time they had all forecast, and for which they had pretended to envy me.

★

Luckily I did not return to Geraldton for a second term. My father, who was beginning to make his reputation at this time, and was becoming prominent in a field in which good men were scarce, received an offer to manage a property, the Cassalis, in Victoria, and we left Lawlers to return to Melbourne where we stayed with Granny while the house in Cassalis was being got ready for us.

This was an experience which I have never forgotten. My grandmother, then a widow, shared a house in Toorak with Uncle Rache. He was a figure whom, through anecdote, for we had seen little of him, we had all been taught to admire.

In appearance he was tall; he dressed elegantly, and was very handsome, he smelt delicious, and he was extremely affable. He played the piano and sang comic songs to us children. He had a yacht and took us sailing.

All this earned our respect and liking, but he also had our admiration and a due sense of awe. Father had told us that when Uncle Rache was young he had run away to sea. He had been gone two years and had circumnavigated the globe, in the course of which he had twice rounded the Horn. The indented fine scar he had on his cheek-bone came from a fight with a sailor. Uncle Rache was thus a romantic figure, and he made my father, with his one eye side-slanted, his lesser height, his smaller, slender build, seem considerably less exciting.

His past was romantic enough. He had been engaged to marry a girl who had been killed while out hunting with him. After a year or two he had married someone whom I remembered dimly as Aunt Maria;

remembered, never saw, because in the year before, while we were at Lawlers, she had suddenly died, and I had not forgotten my mother coming into our room as Laura was putting us to bed, drawing the blinds against the hot desert air, and telling us that Aunt Maria had passed away, and that we must say a special prayer for her.

When we arrived in Melbourne on our way to Cassalis, Uncle Rache was just recovering from his period of mourning. This was the first death I had had experience of, outside books, and I expected him to be very sad. On the contrary, he seemed in the best of spirits, and this gave the first shock of excitement. He appeared to be dining out nearly every night. He would come into the bedroom which Clive and I shared, dressed in evening clothes, his studs and links sparkling in the bedroom light, shedding on our pyjama-clad figures a shining radiance of luxury. He would sit on the end of our beds, telling us stories, and teasing us about the things nearest to our hearts. When he left he would not kiss us good-night. He would merely jump up from the end of the bed, press our foreheads with his hand, or tweak our ears, say 'Good-night, larrikins,' or some such phrase that was unexpected and somehow flattering, and leave us in a glow to sink into sleep.

I think he had something to do with my father's move to Cassalis. Uncle Rache was a stockbroker. Although he was not a technician like my father, he was interested in gold mines, as most business men in Australia were at that time. When we finally moved to Cassalis he was a frequent visitor. He never came without gifts, but the greatest pleasure he brought us all, to my father and mother, as well as to Clive and me, was the impact of his entirely charming personality.

Cassalis remains a poignant memory of my life. Here, although we stayed for less than a year, I grew to boyhood. It came upon me suddenly, and babyhood was laid aside like a suit of clothes out of which one has grown. I was not to change again in spirit until I was seventeen. Here, in the Australian Alps at the age of seven, a season of my life began.

The mine lay in a valley with a hill rising steeply behind the house, a river fed from glacial streams flowing in front, sometimes a mere trickle like the rivers in Italy in summer, sometimes a seething flood, and across a meadow or two the hills rising again, steep grassy slopes at first, merging in the middle background into perpendicular rocky crags which were crowned with snow in the winter, and were wet and brown in the summer. Mitta and Rene had been left at boarding-school in Melbourne, Clive was too young to be put forth in the world. But not I. Luckily, however, no convent this time. About six miles from the house, along the valley, was a school, and thither on the back of a pony I repaired each day by myself. I was very proud of my independence. I could have learnt very little in the school, but no educational establishment I was to attend in the next twenty years was to give me as pure and memorable a delight as that small wooden building, standing in this Alpine valley, with a meadow next to it in which I unsaddled my pony and left him with others to forage all day. I grew to love that pony, and he grew, as is the way of ponies with young owners everywhere, to love me too. When the time came for us to part, I wept at a solitary leave-taking, pressing my yearning face to his neck, and prayed that his new owners would love him as I had done. My father had paid five pounds for him, saddle included. I do not know what he was sold for, but I suppose for about the same sum. I loved him as I loved the members of my own family. It did not seem outrageous that he should sell for so little; it was only heartbreaking that we should have to part.

CHAPTER TWO

My father was being attracted by bigger offers elsewhere. When he died in 1935 a box of his letters came to me, and looking at those which pertain to this period, I see what chances were opened before him in these years when he was still young, when his opinion could make or break a property, but he was still modest about his powers and reputation.

An offer which attracted him particularly was one from the London-Rhodesian Mining & Land Corporation to become their chief Consulting Engineer in Rhodesia where they owned several large mining properties, including the Giant mine, the Cam and Motor, and the Globe and Phoenix.

Sir Thomas Rose, the Comptroller of the Royal Mint in London, though at that time he had never met him, had been impressed by certain papers my father had written for the mining magazines, and had recommended the directors of the London-Rhodesian to consider him for what was a highly paid post with very comfortable conditions. In the end he was given the appointment, and in the spring of 1909, after leaving Mitta and Rene in a boarding-school in Melbourne, we sailed from Melbourne for Cape Town, arriving there at the end of March.

★

I remember Cape Town, a large hotel, and an ocean breaking on the shore just below our windows. The thunder of surf was like the mill stamps to the noise of which we had been put to sleep all our lives. We walked in the close streets, glad to be exercising our land-legs after three weeks on board. There was a new smell to the land, different from Australia; a new light in the sky, black faces pressing in on us in thousands, different from the aborigines, kindlier, friendlier, more intelligent. They smiled at us and we smiled back.

The house which we had been given in Salisbury was a large single-storey one with a verandah, called a stoep, running round three sides of it, and set in a lovely garden in which everything seemed to grow. At the back of the house, about thirty yards away, were the servants' quarters, a series of little cabins with brick floors, quite cool and comfortable, where there lived not only the five servants employed in the house and the two gardeners and the groom, but a large batch of the relatives of each. I suppose that there must have been thirty or forty people living either in or outside these quarters all the time. They used to come and go. They were bush Kaffirs; they wore loin-cloths and blankets, they had not graduated to the dignity of pants, and were altogether of a lower order than Raymond, the house butler, who wore not only trousers but a coat of white linen, or the cook, who wore trousers and a white singlet. But they were of their tribe; they had claims of hospitality and kinship on Raymond and Cook, and they came to visit, to stare, and to eat my father's food. During the day I used to see them leaning against the walls of the cabins, their blankets shed, their black bodies almost naked to the fierce sun, except that they followed

the shade round the cabins. In the early morning, if I
went into the garden, I would see them huddled in their
blankets, and listen amazed to a chorus of snores, and
stand marvelling at the pungent smell of them. Clive
and I used to hear the murmur of their voices when we
had gone to bed and our parents were on the other side
of the house. It was a comforting sound in the African
night.

Very different were the three well-trained servants,
Raymond the butler, the cook and the gardener. They
were the only three to be dignified by the use of
Christian names. The other servants, recognized as
employees not as visitors, whether indoor workers or
out, were known by the amount of wages they earned,
shilling, sixpence, and tickie, which was threepence, and
even half-penny. The indoor servants consisted of a
house-boy, who made the beds and swept, and helped
Raymond serve at table, a laundry-boy who did all the
household washing, and a sort of Tweeny, rank of
Tickie, size and intelligence both proportionately small,
who helped the cook and took away the empty dishes
from outside the dining-room door, and whose apprehensive monkey face could occasionally be glimpsed as
he sat peeling vegetables on the back stoep, or peered
anxiously into the dining-room from the shadows of
the hall.

How the garden came to be made I do not know.
It was beautifully landscaped, the work of some earlier
occupant of my father's position who had experience
or a taste for these things. There were apricot and
guava and mango and mulberry trees, an orchard heavy
and sometimes overpoweringly sweet-smelling with the
odour of ripe, soft fruit; there was an English garden,

with its permanent border, its rose-beds, its sloping
lawn set with trees. There was a wild tropical garden
with artificial rocks to simulate African mountains, and
mysterious plants springing sparsely and rigidly from
the dry sandy soil. The house lay in the midst of this
profusion, and from the warm stoep where we sat
behind pillars we could watch Charlie, the head gardener, and his two bare-bodied, bare-footed assistants
at work all day. Salisbury lies 5000 feet above sea-
level, and although it is only ten degrees off the equator,
the nights on that great upper plain on which it lies
can be cool, however fierce the heat in the middle
of the day. The rainfall is tropical in intensity
during the rainy season, almost nothing for the other
nine months of the year. The air is clear, pellucid,
strong in the early morning and just before night falls,
with its common effect of a curtain of black rushing
down. As the day advances the air starts to shimmer
with heat; at midday it is heavy and listless, but as the
day declines a little breeze whispers and stirs, the smell
comes back into things, people begin to move after
their siestas, the tedium for a boy while the world was
hot and slept is dissolved. The first sign of returning
life came always, I remember, from the garden.
Charlie's boys would commence to wheel great clank-
ing cans of water from the stables to the garden; and
with the fresh scent of revived things brought quickly
to life by the touch of cool water, my own spirits would
lift and I would look forward to the adventure of the
evening.

I was to be put at the Alfred Beit School which was
newly built and had just been opened by the Duke of
Connaught. The little I had known of big school life,

the convent at Geraldton, had led me to distrust it; the
little building near Cassalis had been a different matter.
You could get to know thirty or forty boys, but three
or four hundred! But I was caught up in the damned
system and had to submit.

My mother drove with me to be interviewed by
Mr. Grant. He appeared not so formidable as I had
feared. He and my mother laughed and talked above
my head. Though my worst suspicions had not been
confirmed, I was not for relaxing any vigilance, and I
was furious with my mother for neglecting to be watchful. I heard her ask Mr. Grant to call on us and meet
my father. In due course he came to dinner. He came
often subsequently, and gradually I learnt to accept him.
But I could never forget, as the others naturally could,
that beneath his smiling face lay hidden a tiger,
capable as headmaster, so the boys whispered, of the
greatest ferocity.

He had a small neat figure and even I could see that
he was handsome. He had an attractive voice, and
laughed with my mother a good deal over jokes beyond
me, beyond even worth trying to understand. I
thought how much alike they looked, and how very
pretty my mother was when she smiled. Mr. Grant
must have thought so, too, for he was always making
her blush and smile.

My mother was then thirty-five, and I think at the
ripest point of her life. She had a great sense of gaiety
and an untiring energy. Her house was run for her by
the competent Raymond; she had nothing more to do
than to discuss with him at the beginning of each day
what her programme was to be; he saw to the rest.
With two of her children away at boarding-school, and

Clive and I little trouble, for the first time in her life she could revel in her happiness. And for those few years she was very happy.

She played golf, she shot, she rode, she entertained and was entertained constantly. Our stoep at sundown became crowded with people of her and my father's age. I would sometimes sit on the stoep with my bare legs over the side, the heated stone sending a pleasant warmth up the calves of my legs. Above me I could hear their voices, smell the evening and the pungent scent of Turkish cigarettes, hear the clink of ice in glasses, and turn and see them if I so cared, women who sometimes wore small revolvers strapped to their waists, women of all sizes and with all kinds of voices, and men not all as neat and good-looking as Mr. Grant. My mother shone amongst them, and it was not because she was mine that I thought so. When I turned to look I could see that she was the centre of attraction, and it depended on the mood of the small boy sitting on the warm stone in the evening light whether he was proud of her or jealous of the others.

Harry, a nephew of Raymond, fresh from a mission school, was ordained into the office of my boy. He was bigger than myself, being three years older, and he was bare except for a pair of drill trousers into which he had been promoted in order to come into the house. He was under the general surveillance of Raymond. He spoke only a little mission English and Raymond spoke to him the curious clicking tongue of their tribe. My father explained to me that I was to be as responsible for Harry as Harry was for me; we were to keep each other out of mischief and out of the sun. Harry would know how to deal with snakes and would see that I got

home from school without dawdling along the hot
dusty road. I could teach him English, and he could
teach me Mashona. Anyhow it was the arrangement,
concluded my father, patting me on the head and
ordering me to be a good boy, his usual sign of dismissal. Raymond must have been clicking off the same
instructions to Harry. He, too, finished with a paternal
smile; and then we were left to get to know each other.

Harry regarded me with hard suspicion, but I looked
at him with eager interest. I felt as I did when I was
given a new toy and told to be very careful with it.
We did not attempt at first to communicate with
Harry's little store of English. Anyhow, swept suddenly from the quarters at the back into the big house, I
doubt whether he could have spoken. We made our
way instead through the house to the garden, and began
our friendship with only our eyes to help us.

School was from 8.30 in the morning till 1.30. It
went through with only a short break for those five
hours, after which in the heat of the day all Africa slept.
Harry came down with me each morning, and was
waiting for me with the other boys under the shade of
a tree when we came out of school at 1.30. He carried
a large plantain leaf which he used to protect me
against the sun, and to keep flies off himself. After
lunch and the long boring siesta, I would come out into
the garden about four when the first hint of the evening
cool would be touching the air. From then on was
playtime, and hours of delight and interest which I can
remember vividly after fifty years. With Harry I must
have been allowed to go anywhere. We would sometimes just play in the garden, sometimes at the house of
a friend, sometimes wander to the banks of the Hunyani

which flowed yellow and thick a few miles from Salisbury, where we would see crocodiles sleeping on the banks and sometimes hippos floating on the surface of the water, and throw stones at them to disturb them. He taught me a great deal about nature, and some Mashona words of which I was very proud, most of the other white people speaking only kitchen-Kaffir where the words were pronounced like English words, not with the rapid-fire effect of the real Mashona.

Harry was sure to have me back well before sunset because at that hour the natives fed. Their diet was very simple, mealie from a pot around which they all settled on their haunches, reaching in their black hands, taking out the sticky substance in enormous handfuls which they rolled into the shape of small buns, and dipping those as they ate into a communal plate of gravy before stuffing them into their mouths. After all these years I can hear the sticky sound as they rolled the mealie meal in their hands, the grunts and noise of their eating. I was not supposed to be there watching them and Raymond dismissed me when he caught me. But Harry had made me free of these quarters, and nobody had power to command me to go away except Raymond.

There were other white boys and girls, the children of my parents' friends, whom I got to know at school. I remember that they sometimes came to our garden, and that sometimes we were commanded by our parents to go to theirs. But I made no friends. I was always anxious to be rid of them, and be alone with Harry again. All I can remember of that period is Harry's face; he became for me the mirror into which I gazed wonderingly, and what I discovered and comprehended of the confusing but fascinating world about me, I learned at this stage from that strange, primitive source. I admired him for his strength and wisdom and certitude. I trusted him blindly, and ceased to develop these qualities in myself, as I might have done, left to fend for myself and to learn from harsh experience.

Once, in the garden in the early morning, when the mist was just lifting from the fruit trees, and the front of the house was silent and in shadow, the back yellow with morning light and noisy with the stir of black sleepers awakening to the world, we found a cobra coiled round a little hut where garden chairs were stacked at night. It was so long and fat that its coils went twice round the little hut. Scaly, black, immense, it bulged with life and menace. I stood paralysed with fright, but Harry said, 'Where is its head?' and instead of running away or remaining taut with fright as I was, he tiptoed round the little hut until he saw the great hooded head rise from among the coils, waving drunkenly from side to side, trembling on that great repulsive body, reared to strike. Then Harry told me to stand still, and pattered back along the path to the servants' kraal, and in a few moments was back with half a dozen natives, armed with nothing more than axes and knives. They obeyed Harry's instructions as recruits obey a sergeant-major, watching him with their large eyes, moving to their appointed places a few feet apart at his clicking, soft-spoken commands. Then at a signal they all struck at once with a mighty shout, axes and knives cutting the writhing mass into half a dozen pieces, while at the same moment Harry with an iron bar leapt forward and struck at the back of the snake's head. There followed a moment of dancing and breathing as they hit at the writhing remains, shouting at the tops of their voices, while I stood there, my frozen fright melting in the reflected heat of their triumph, until Raymond, followed by my mother, came running down the path to find the cause of this disorder. My mother looked at me with her large and beautiful eyes full of wonder and apprehension, and drew me against her. I told her that Harry had found the snake, and that he had helped to kill it. 'He should have brought you back first,' she said, and Harry hung his head, not understanding what was said but conscious that he was disapproved of.

'But Harry was brave. You don't understand. The snake might have killed anyone coming here, but Harry found it and it was he who got it killed.'

'Master Rache is right,' said Raymond, and put his hand on Harry's shoulder. I can remember now the look of adulation on Harry's face as Raymond touched him.

The servants, chattering to themselves, were carrying the snake away to their quarters in buckets, and after one proud glance at his uncle, Harry scuttled after them, and I was left to walk back along the path with my mother's arm round my shoulders, when what I longed for was to be with Harry, far away from the interfering adult world.

I do not think that he felt for me what I felt for him, but I was his charge and that gave him status in the natives' kraal. But I think he had larger ambitions which he did not see a chance of satisfying as long as he was attached to me. I tethered him to my nursery age; he wanted to soar into the adult world, and he wanted chiefly to be attached to the stables, or to the motor-car, this last in the charge of a gap-toothed expert named

D

Gerenko, who certainly led the most novel and continuously exciting life of any native in the kraal.

How he came by the job I do not know. He must have been a stable-hand who was bad with horses, but could not be sacked because his relationship to Raymond or Cook, who governed the affairs of this little community, gave him some preferment or hereditament of which nobody could deprive him. He was accepted as an authority by a whole drift of underboys who sat on their haunches at his feet, while he himself sat on a packing-box under the shade of a giant mulberry tree which flowered outside the stables, and here he held forth endlessly on subjects sufficiently interesting for the others to squat there by the hour, swatting at their necks and backs with long plantain leaves to kill the flies, turning to one another with little undertones of chattering while Gerenko boomed interminably above. He must have had a reputation for being witty, for every now and then in his unending discourse his voice would assume a falsetto chatter or, it might be, a deep liturgical boom, whereupon his audience would cease to swat the flies, and as likely as not swat each other, while cackles of laughter rose up under the mulberry tree, and Gerenko's enormous lips would slide slowly apart in a self-satisfied grin, and the place where his teeth should have been would appear, and he would scratch his head wonderingly and mutter to himself with pleasure.

Gerenko had time to be a garden philosopher because his duties, though absorbing, were simple, and could for the most part be performed well away from the sight of authority. He was the car-boy.

My father, with typical extravagance, had bought a Willys-Overland car soon after we came to Salisbury in 1909. There were only dirt roads in Salisbury, and rough tracks in the bush outside. One could go even less far here than we had been able to go in the desert of Western Australia with the horseless carriage three years before. On the other hand, this was a much more splendid conveyance than that had been. It was heavy with brass trimmings, and had carbide headlights to make night driving possible, and an engine whose horse-power I remember was always being quoted. Gerenko was promoted from the stables to the brick garage my father had had built for the car in the garden. Gerenko must have been the envy and admiration of almost the entire Kaffir population of Salisbury, who treated him with the reverence and respect due to a witch-doctor. But it was a horrid job. It was all right as long as the car was in the garage, and he had only to wash it and polish its brass. But when it came time to start it up, he was the man who had to crank it. The car's starting-handle kicked like a mule and Gerenko had to jump clear, holding his wrist, groaning audibly with pain after each swing when contact was made. When it did start, when it did not die away as it so often did, but continued to rev, then the Kaffirs regarded Gerenko with awe, and he assumed an air of solemnity becoming to one who has just performed a miracle, walking round with a pleased strut until my father had to call him to get aboard. He had to accompany the car wherever it went, since no one could start it except him. He could not sit in the car with the other occupants, and he could not run behind. His fate was to lie face downwards on the running-board, his enormous toe gripping in a pre-hensile way the handle of the back door and his arm thrust through the spare tyre at the front of the running-board to prevent his falling off. When we got to the end of whatever journey we were taking, he would tumble into the dust, and rise bowing and smiling, his black face a mask of fine white dust, spitting and snuffling, stamping his large feet to get the circulation back into his legs, shaking both from the vibration of the car and from pride in his ownership of it.

His greatest glory was when it was used occasionally at night and the carbide lamps had to be prepared in the afternoon. Then, surrounded by the shiftless and jobless members of the servants' quarters, and others momentarily Absent without Leave from their proper occupations, and generally by Harry and me, he would pour out a pile of the white powder, pour water over it, and stand back like a chemist in some laboratory as the hissing, pungent cloud of steam shot into the air, not unconscious, I think, of the 'Oohs' and 'Aahs' of admiration from his audience.

His greatest shame was when the car broke down, and neither he nor my father nor anyone who was with us could get it going again, and he would have to run back to summon the horses to rescue us. These occasions were not infrequent, so Gerenko's activities were geared to a pitch of either ecstasy or despair, punctuated with hours he might have used for meditation had not his unique job given him a reputation for wisdom, and had not the position of the garage, handily shady and secluded from the house, made it an inviting place for the idle and the unattached to come and squat on their haunches and listen to the great man pouring out wisdom as he polished his brass.

★

Gerenko had the car out one morning. My mother
was to drive me to keep my first appointment with a
dentist. A tooth had to come out, professionally, not
by the door-handle method.

The dentist, Dr. Cleveland, knew my mother. It
was a bright sunny morning just after the rains, and the
curtains in his room were lifting gently in the breeze.
I looked with interest at the little round glass table, the
enormous chair and all the silver instruments, while my
mother and Dr. Cleveland exchanged laughter and
chatter in high-pitched, uncertain, unordinary voices I
noticed grown-up people always used when they first
met. I never listened to the words, I only heard the
sound.

I climbed into the chair and was hoisted into position
by Dr. Cleveland, and was at once aware that something
unexpected was to happen, and both Dr. Cleveland and
my mother were anxious about its effect on me. Dr.
Cleveland's large pale face, his pale-blue eyes behind a
pair of rimless pince-nez glasses he wore, was very close
to mine; and standing on the other side of the chair
was my mother. I noticed her hands clasped in front
of her, a physical sign of anxiety instinctive with her
and easily recognizable to me, who knew her every
gesture. Suddenly alarmed, I decided not to co-operate.

It was slow work getting me to open my mouth,
and then impossible to get me to acknowledge which
tooth it was in trouble. Finally the tooth was found
rocking on its foundations, and Dr. Cleveland smiled
an unmirthful smile and said he would fix that in a
jiffy. While he was preparing something with his back
turned, I shot at my mother an imploring look, putting
into it all the love for her and trust in her that I had

accumulated in the few years of my life. I beseeched
her with that look to release me from the power of this
wicked man in the white coat, with his great white face
and glasses, and take me home, where in love and with
laughter, and for no more reward than a kiss, we would
do again what we had done in the past, a piece of cotton,
the brass door-handle, the preliminary threatening
swing, then pouff! a sharp taste of blood that flowed
no more quickly than the immense sense of relief, and
a white tooth swinging wildly at the end of the cotton.
Why this stranger instead ? Why did he intrude ?

All this I asked my mother with my hot imploring
eyes, and she understood all.

'I think I'll leave him with you, Dr. Cleveland,' she
said. 'I'll come back in ten minutes. Be brave, my
darling.'

She squeezed my hand and I heard her behind me,
rushing from the room. Dr. Cleveland turned and
smiled broadly at me, trying the conspiratorial approach.

'Come on, old chap. We'll have it out in a jiffy,
and I'll give you a beautiful box to put it in. Women
can't bear the sight of men being brave.'

I opened my mouth unwillingly, but panic seized
me when he put the forceps in my mouth. I thought I
would choke, squirmed violently and felt the corner of my
mouth bruised by his hand. Since he showed no sign
of withdrawal, I quickly and forcibly bit it. He started
back with a jump, and looked at me in an angry way.

He called in the nurse who had been working at the
desk in the hall when we arrived. Then, while she held
my hands and he stood behind me, he got me to open
my mouth long enough to insert a gag, and the forceps
were soon exploring in their cold, solid, antiseptic way

my small hot mouth. When they finally found the tooth, I kicked Dr. Cleveland's little glass table with all my might, sending it, and everything on it, toppling to the floor. My strangled cries now competed with Dr. Cleveland's heavy breathing. When he started to pull I kicked him in the stomach, and he paused a moment and looked at me venomously, and said he would have to tie my legs if I wasn't careful.

He then took me under the arms and lifted me from the chair and sat me on the floor. He reached for a cushion from a sofa that was just by us and pressed my head down on it. Then he put a knee on my one arm, fought off the other with his elbow, allowed my legs to kick freely and unrestricted, reached for the tooth; and in a minute it was all over. Then he got up and said, 'Go and spit out the blood,' and weeping I went to the basin and spat and sobbed into it, and tried to remember the outrage that had been done to me. But triumph kept breaking in. My tooth was out, and not by any babyish work with cotton and door-handle, but taken out by a dentist. Before me now lay all the pleasures of ice-cream and cake, and a drive home in the motor. I sobbed quietly, sweet tears of joy at the beauty of the world, the white curtains lifting in the breeze, the scent of morning outside, the lovely day before me.

This was my world and my background at a time when the process of growth was accelerating in me, and the kind of being I was one day to be was beginning to be shaped under this African sun and in such company. To my parents, in the flush and happiness of their own lives, I was a child still, and they no doubt felt that they had done all that was necessary in providing someone like Harry to keep me from accidents when I was outside the house. At other hours I was safe at school, and in the evenings they always spared time for that open display of love which I remember now with such happiness. But they did not notice, or if they did, paid no attention to the development in me of those feelings of jealousy and vanity, pride and selfishness which now began to grow in my infant psyche. In large families these little shoots are nipped as they appear, or if they grow too large, by the frank criticism of others; but solitary children, like plants in a conservatory, can grow them to a disastrous degree. I was not only a solitary child, I was a flattered one. Harry's obedience might have been fatal for me, but I was saved by the fact that he was not as fond of me as I was of him, and away from the house he could take command and become the leader. I strove to win his affection, and found that I had one way of holding his attention. He loved a story, the more fanciful the better. No one ever had a more rapt listener than I had in him, and I strove to hold him with tales which I invented. It gave me a sense of power to be able to do this, especially when I found how effective a means of holding Harry's attention, of getting him to do what I wanted to do, was the element of surprise in a story. I would stop at a certain point. 'What happen?' Harry would say.

'I'll tell you tomorrow.'

'No, tell me now. What happen?'

'It's a secret until tomorrow,' I would reply, knowing that I had Harry at my complete command while the *dénouement* of the story remained to be unfolded.

I began at times when I was not with him to invent characters and stories, putting them aside in my memory for later use. Most children have vivid imaginations, but mine I overworked and got a strong pleasure from my own stories.

A shadow crept into my life; for the first time I knew the sickening pangs of jealousy.

When we went to Lawlers three years before, a young mining engineer who was to be assistant to my father was living in the house. The previous manager had been a bachelor, and Mike Drummond, as this young man was called, had shared the manager's quarters with him, and had been looked after by Keno.

Mike Drummond was the son of a well-to-do manufacturer of dairy products in Adelaide. He was at that time in his late twenties, a good-looking, dark-haired, red-faced young man with a broad, noble expanse of white brow, where his cork helmet shaded his forehead from the sun. I suppose that he had been prepared to move out when our large family cavalcade arrived in Lawlers. But the house was capacious and he charmed us all. I expect that he stayed on for a few days to see us settled, the stay extended until finally it was accepted that he should continue to live with us. He was the first to call my father Chief, probably because he could not call him Gordon. My mother he called, as everyone did, Joey. To us children he was like an elder brother. He had a fine baritone voice, and could sing not only the sentimental drawing-room ballads of the day, 'Asleep in the Deep', 'Thora', 'Absent' and others like that, but old Scottish songs which by their simplicity and poignancy wrung tears from us, proud as we were of our Scottish ancestry. He and my father sang duets, my father's thin but very clear and beautiful tenor voice playing like a swallow in the evening sky against the pure melody of Mike's rich baritone.

My father must have been fond of him because when we went to Rhodesia he arranged a job for him in the London-Rhodesian Company's office in Salisbury, and we had not been there many months before Mike arrived from Australia to join us. By this time he had become as much a member of the family as we who had been born in it, and so he was to remain until my mother's death. Everyone loved him and he loved all of us. If there was a reservation on either side, it was in his feelings for me and in mine for him. I see now that he was as jealous of me as I was of him.

He was a man and he was much cleverer at hiding his feelings than I, his opponent, who was used to being the centre of my mother's attention. Above my head, at the level of communication which grown-ups use with one another, thinking themselves not understood by the child who listens, there was some amusement at my petulance and at my occasional bad behaviour towards Mike, which was correctly diagnosed but improperly treated. I understood what went on, and I think Mike knew that I did, although neither he nor my mother guessed with what a sharp stroke of agony I caught sometimes, in a room full of talk and laughter, a note in my mother's voice or his which had once sounded only between my mother and me.

The house in Salisbury had a wing thrown out at the back extending from a long passage that led to the kitchen. This had been built onto the house at some

later date than its original construction. Here Mike
slept and had his own private quarters, with a separate
entrance. But he always took his meals with us, and
was looked after by our servants, and the evenings he
spent in our drawing-room, from where, night after
night, the sound of music and the familiar comfortable
clatter of the grown-up world would put me to sleep.

My father's office was in the Company Headquarters
at Salisbury, but as Consulting Engineer to the company
he had to visit all the mines, of which there were at that
time five, and also to examine any new claims or
properties offered to the company. He was often on
the move, and away from home for two or three weeks
at a time.

Clive, who had been ill a great deal with whooping-
cough and pleurisy ever since coming to Rhodesia and
had spent a lot of time in bed, was sufficiently con-
valescent to accompany my father on one excursion,
and I remained alone with my mother at home. I was
allowed to remove from the bedroom I usually shared
with Clive and sleep in the dressing-room which ad-
joined my mother's bedroom. I was to be permitted to
stay up for dinner each night. We planned to have the
dishes we each liked the best. Instead of Dickens,
which my father had for years been reading to me every
night, because I was entranced by him, she was to tell
me stories of her childhood in the mountains of Australia. Mike also was to be away, and with the house to
ourselves, we were to have private hours together which
promised every delight. My imagination leapt ahead

to pleasures and excitements so unprecedented, so beyond any yet experienced, that I could hardly wait for us to be left alone, and was impatient for everyone to be off.

But when the moment came and the first night we sat together, the lamp on the table burning between us, my stomach distended with the meal I had just devoured, I was tortured by an overpowering somnolence and an aching anxiety that my mother might find herself bored being left alone with me, and send me off to bed and bury herself in the pages of a book. But the sleepiness passed, my spirits aroused themselves and she told me of what it was like when she was young, a period so remote that I would have credited a world in which there were two-headed giants and people lived on locusts and wild honey instead of porridge, chops and cheese. But it was not with such wonders that I was entertained, events exciting enough, I suppose, in which my legendary uncles had participated. What held me rapt was my mother's face, beautiful as a rose upon a stem, smiling in recollection and animated with memories of long ago. What excited me was not what she said but the fact that she spoke only to me, that we were alone in the house, the lamplight enclosing us in a warm circle which nothing could break. Except time itself. The clock was the only threat, ticking away on the mantelpiece. But on this night even its threat was muted. I might have to go ahead to bed. Maybe my mother would sit on here for a little. But the click of her knitting-needles would be heard by me in my new bedroom across the hall. And if I stayed awake, I would hear her come to bed. The door would be open between our two rooms. I would see across the black-

ness the light cast by her lamp, hear the movements
she made as she prepared for bed, and when the light
was finally put out there we would be, within a few
yards of each other, sharing the intimate warm darkness,
the world safely shut outside.

I remember that my mother asked me that evening
what I would like to be when I grew up. I replied, 'A
priest,' and she said quickly with a little laugh, 'Oh, but
you can't be that.' I was momentarily shocked. We
still had family prayers every morning, we still said
grace before each meal, we spoke of God without embarrassment. He was a real presence to all of us. I
think I must have said that I would become a priest
chiefly to please my mother, to make this night memorable above all for her, to make her love for me as over-
whelming as mine was for her. Her laughing dismissal
of the plan left me startled. Until we discovered that
she thought I had said 'police', and we rocked with
laughter at the misunderstanding, though it seemed
a splendid thing, too, to be a policeman, but at least
my mother's refusal to consider that did not shock
me. What fun we had that evening before the time
came, half an hour later than usual, when I was sent off
to bed.

I had fallen asleep before my mother came. I do not
know what sound it was that woke me. I only know
that suddenly I was wide awake and conscious that
something was threatening. I cried out to my mother,
my heart thumping in my chest, my mouth dry with
terror. There was no reply; there was only an instant's
silence, then the sound of bare feet — the feet of a Kaffir
— bounding across the floor. Then there was no sound,
and I imagined her lying there dead, and no one else in

the house. Sick with terror, I got out of bed. A patch where the darkness was not complete showed the door open between our rooms. I felt my way to this, still calling to her, and saw against the outline of the night her dressing-table suddenly shoved aside, and the figure of a man jumping through the bow windows. Between that dim luminosity and me floated a well of inky darkness, and somewhere in that well my mother's bed, and her upon it. I crept towards it, crying 'Mother, Mother !' and felt the brass upright rails at the end, felt my way round by hand, and felt her body. She moved slightly as I touched her, and then I heard her sigh like someone just recovering consciousness. I heard the rattle of a box of matches. She struck a light, and there was my mother looking at me with distended, frightened eyes, but alive.

When the lamp was lit she sat on the edge of the bed, holding me in her arms. I was shaking with fright ; she was trembling. She had drawn the curtains before we sat down, but she could not replace the dressing-table, which lay askew, evidence that we had not dreamt all this, but had lived through it. We were alone in the house. This was before the days of telephones or electric light. Outside lay the servants' quarters where reliable people like Raymond slept, but where also in the garden slept thirty or forty members of the tribe, their heads wrapped in blankets. One of these had probably been the intruder, one of these grinning blacks who, swathed in sheet or blanket, watched us with rolling eyes when we walked in the garden by day.

The night stretched before us illimitable and threatening, and paralysed with fright we could not move. After a little my mother, holding the lamp in one hand

and with the other round my shoulders, led me along
the passage to the bathroom. There she poured the
bath full of hot water, undressed me, and set me in it.
As I sat there, as she lifted the sponge, continually
squeezing the warm water over my shoulders, my ague
gradually died down, but the fright had stiffened the
very marrow in my bones, even the jelly in my skull,
so that I had to keep wrinkling my forehead and feeling
with my hand the top of my head to make sure that it
was still a part of me, and a terrible feeling of melancholy poured in to fill the vacuum left by my departing
fright. My mother looked at me with anxious eyes and
for the first time I could not respond. For the first time
in my life I felt completely alone.

That night left a mark on me which it took years
to erase. I not only dreaded the dark. I was afraid
of the night even when the lamps were lit. I could
not be left alone when I was put to bed. Not even
Clive's presence in the room helped. Someone had
to sit with me until I fell asleep. And it could not be
one of the boys; I could not trust them. It must be
my mother or my father, and sometimes when I woke
and found them gone I screamed, awakening Clive,
disordering the serving of dinner, bringing my father
or my mother running from the drawing-room. I did
not know until long afterwards what an effect I was
having on their lives. They had been used to dining
out a great deal, and to entertaining in return. For a
month or two after my experience they were not able
to do even this. I do not know how it would all have

ended had my father not become suddenly ill with amoebic dysentery, and attention was shifted dramatically from me to him.

It happened that old Dr. Appleyard, whose house was separated from ours only by a rough field in which a donkey grazed, was on the point of retiring. He had taken in as his young partner that year a Dr. Godfrey Huggins, who had just come out from England; and it was this fair-haired, blue-eyed young man, one day to become Prime Minister of Rhodesia, who on a red Indian motor-cycle swept up our drive two or three times each day to attend to my father. Clive and I, with Harry generally in attendance, began to watch out for him because he gave us such a friendly smile whenever he saw us. We also wanted to look at the motorbike at close quarters.

Mike moved out, and two nurses, one for the day and one for the night, moved in to his quarters, and my father fought out his desperate struggle for life. Six weeks after he had first been stricken with the illness his temperature dropped and he turned back from death to face life again. My mother, worn out by anxiety, badly needed a rest, and as my father's slow recovery quickened its pace, although he could not be moved, it was decided that she should take Clive and me to stay on one of the company's tobacco farms at Marandellas, about forty-six miles south-east of Salisbury.

We went there by train. The day was fresh, the countryside strange, the engine old-fashioned and primitive even for those days. These all gave the journey an interest which I have never forgotten. There were not many white passengers on the train, but the open iron trucks in which the Kaffirs travelled were crowded with natives going back to their tribal homes after earning enough in the town. They were very cheerful, and the sound of their chattering voices rose even above the noise of the engine and the grind of the wheels on the track. The engine burned wood, not coal, and at intervals throughout the day we stopped, the natives jumped down from the trucks and formed a line to pass up the wood like railway sleepers that lay stacked twenty yards or so from the tracks. These were flung into the boiler or loaded onto the tender.

We were passing through hilly wooded country, sage-green in colour. We were told by experienced passengers who talked to us that this was lion country, and that they could generally be heard when the train stopped at night. The train was bound for Gwelo, about one hundred and eighty miles to the south-west, where it would join the main line for the Cape. This was a journey of several days at the rate we were travelling, but it would take us only to the late afternoon to reach Marandellas. Would there be lions there, I wanted to know? There would be lions there, the man told us, plenty of them. 'Man-eaters?' I asked. 'Yes, man-eaters,' he said. 'You had better watch out.'

I shivered with anticipation. I was afraid of no animal. It was only the dark and people that I had come to fear. The sound of an animal in the night was an assurance of something living that meant me no harm. But I hadn't heard a lion roar.

We reached Marandellas that afternoon about four and were met by the manager of the farm, who lived alone with his wife in this remote station, farming 10,000 acres and managing 2000 natives. They were pleased to have visitors. The farmhouse was a well-

E

built one on the rocky side of a kopje looking out over a wide valley in which the tobacco fields lay. At this time of the year they were green stalks just starting to turn yellow, and from the farmhouse up above it was like looking down on a swirling sea as the vast fields of tobacco turned and stirred in the wind.

That night as we lay in bed we heard the lions, and I heard the voice of Africa. At first they sounded so close that I was frightened. But the manager came in to explain to us that it was the rocky sides of the hills that gave back the echoes and made the sound seem so close, and that those we heard were probably two or three miles away. They would come closer in the night. I have never heard anything like that sound, impossible to describe, of a lion on the hunt at night. It is quite different from the hungry moan of the lion in captivity in a zoo. It shook the beds on which we lay, and even the farmhouse seemed to shudder and cower away as the majestic noise echoed in roar after roar along the hillside.

After a few minutes the sound did not frighten me. The lion roamed in the night and every other night noise of bird or animal or creak of building seemed to hush with respect for the moment while the king padded by on his tremendous paws, and I imagined his long tail whipping from side to side with irritable authority. After a moment the shattering roar even brought comfort, and the feeling that there was a guardian in the night, and I drifted into a dreamless sleep as the hills echoed to the thunder.

★

At about this time I was sent with my brother Clive to board at Mr. Grant's school while my father and mother made a journey to England. This was undertaken partly for my father's convalescence but also, we learnt later, so that he could make arrangements to terminate his engagement in Rhodesia. The climate plainly did not suit him. Besides, he and my mother had at that time, although we children did not know it, a private anxiety about her health. My father wished to consult a London specialist, and he wanted to arrange schools for us in England.

So the house in Salisbury was shut up and left in the charge of Raymond. I said farewell to Harry, and hated him because he did not feel the parting as I did. Mitta and Rene, who had come from Australia to join us about six months before, were sent to a girls' boarding-school in Salisbury. I went with Clive to make the by now customary round of farewells to loved objects, figures and scenes. The parting was to be but brief, a few months at the most. But we boys felt the excitement in the air. We were on the move again. We had never been in any place for very long. It was rapture to move ahead into the unknown; even to live as a boarder at school promised adventure. But small boys guard against mishap by these totemistic observances, and we used to make a great ceremony of saying farewell to our surroundings.

If I expected that Mr. Grant would behave towards us as he did when he came as a visitor to our home, I was in for a shock. He did not treat us harshly, but he was quick to show us that we were not to presume on the fact that he was on intimate terms with our family. I remember attempting to assert my identity, and Mr.

Grant's smiling lack of recognition of the attempt comes back to me after all these years. Clive and I supported each other. We were put in the same dormitory. Thrilled with the novelty of sleeping with so many boys, enraptured with their conversation after lights were put out, we attempted to join in, and could not believe it when we were commanded to shut up. I remember a night when we all sat up discussing what became known as the Agadir incident, and the awful silence that followed my bursting into the conversation with, 'But my father says there is bound to be a war with the Germans, and the sooner it comes the better for the Empire'; and the shameful imitative chatter that burst forth, every boy in the dormitory a born mimic, 'But *my* father says . . .', each one excelling the other in outrageous prophecy until I lay down in bed burning with shame, and wished that my father had kept his opinions to himself and had not infected me with them.

The shades of the prison-house closed round us, the novelty of being with so many other boys lasting but a day or two, and leaving us forlorn in a tumultuous, rowdy world. I was soon called upon to fight, and being anxious to placate the crowd which surrounded me and my opponent, smiled in sickly and servile fashion at them, as we two circled round one another, fists raised to do battle. This had the opposite effect from that at which I had aimed. Those who may have had some sort of sympathy for me, or contempt for my opponent who was larger than I, and had been thrust rather unwillingly into the office of aggressor, were totally and quite rightly alienated by what they took to be my revolting appeal for mercy, and everyone joined in urging my opponent to demolish me without delay. I had never before fought anyone, but I had read lots of books in which fights were described, and I had a general idea of what was required; I was merely reluctant to practise it. I was not afraid of my opponent, but I was very unhappy that so many people plainly disliked me, and it was to mollify them that I had smiled.

Urged on by his supporters, my opponent gave a bellicose grunt and came in and hit me painfully on the nose. My eyes stung, and for a moment I contemplated turning and running away. That was impossible; I was surrounded by a closely packed ring of yelling boys. Pleased with what he had accomplished, my opponent was now dancing about in a pugilistic way. The look of ferocity which he had worn before he hit me had given way to a self-satisfied smirk. Suddenly, beyond him, and just for an instant, I caught a glimpse of Clive on the outside of the ring, crying and wiping his nose on his sleeve. Then I received a smart hit on the tip of my ear, and it burnt with such fire that I thought he must have taken the top off it. I thought to myself, 'I'll murder him, I'll beat him into a bloody pulp. I'll go to prison and be hanged. I would rather die than stay here.'

And with a gesture of despair which, since it involved flinging wide my arms, was the worst possible stance for the action I contemplated, I flung myself at him, battering him with my fists, and at the same time pushing an energetic knee into his stomach, meanwhile grunting and gasping like a man engaged on a herculean task.

It was soon over. Horrified shouts from the spectators, sportsmen to a man; disentanglement of my

writing body from that of my startled opponent who
was now bellowing with pain and outrage; loud de-
claimings of my villainy on everybody's part.   A
master, attracted to the scene by the din, was given an
excited account of what had happened. He listened for
a moment, said briefly, 'Shut up, everybody, and clear
out,' and they went, muttering, and with the same
backward, malevolent glances as the crowd in a play of
Shakespeare's. Clive and I were left alone with him.

He looked at me without sympathy, which wasn't
surprising, but what was worse, without interest. 'Go
and wash your face, and if you must fight again, fight
like a man, not a street arab.'

This incident deepened in me my hatred of school,
communal life. If I had known then how many years
of it lay ahead of me, I think I would have died of
despair. But I didn't know. 'Soon', I thought to
myself, 'Mother will be back, and I can leave this hateful
place, and never come near it again.'

But it was many months before she came, and I can
remember every hour of misery that Clive and I endured in that period. From then on we used evasive
tactics. Whenever we could, we would creep away to
the dining-hall, and sit on a bench at one end of the
room. Sometimes we would talk of home, but not
often because it made us sad. Usually I would read
aloud to Clive, either from one of the books I had
brought with me, or from a novel I was writing.

I had begun this great work a few months before we
came to the school, and I had packed the manuscript in
my tuck-box. I had been, and still was, very proud of
it, and I had promised my mother, who had had to
listen to many readings as the tale unfolded its sinuous

length, that it would be finished when she returned
from England. Now I had little heart and less opportunity to get on with it, but as I was terrified that some
boy might discover it and hold it up to ridicule, I
always took it out of my tuck-box when we stole away
together for these silent sessions. I read it to Clive
several times; he was always sweet-natured and gener-
ous, and used to ask for a helping from this sometimes
in preference to one of our books. Thus, with the balm
of words, we comforted ourselves, hearing in the distance the noise from the play-room, a subdued roar like
animals in a den, where the other boys spent this hour.

One morning on my plate at breakfast-time was a
letter from my mother. If I had read it then, and found
what momentous news it contained, I believe I would
have risen from the table with a great shout of defiance.
But I had become furtive; I put it in my shirt pocket,
told Clive about it on the way out of the room, post-
poning the pleasure of opening it until we could get
away by ourselves later in the day.

My mother wrote that she would be returning alone
the following month; that Father was to stay and work
in London, and that she was coming back only to close
the house and pick us up; that from now on we would
be living in England and going to English schools; that
she had taken a lovely house and that we would be very
happy, and she said that she was longing to see us again.

All our troubles were in that instant washed away.
We could have cried with relief, and I am not sure that
we didn't. The thought of seeing Mother again within
the measure of weeks was overpowering.

★

Farewell now to Africa. Would our wanderings never cease? Pray God not, if it meant our being abandoned again. Once more we were caught up in the delicious excitement of travel, the long train journey to Beira, the last sight of the African coast, the old familiar throb of a ship's engine, family prayers night and morning in Mother's cabin, the radiation of love and beauty from one adored person, peace at night when we laid ourselves down to sleep, joy in the morning at the prospect before us of another day of happiness.

I spared not a backward thought for what I had loved in Africa, for Harry, for the long hot days, for dewy hours in the garden at dawn and in the late afternoon, for the strong roar of those lions at Marandellas, for the hippos sleeping in the Hunyani, and the crocodiles basking on the sunlit sandy spits along the shore. But all this was laid away in my memory, and was to be remembered afterwards. Africa had touched me with its warm golden hand, and its touch left a mark which could never be eradicated.

CHAPTER THREE

THE England to which we came in the early summer of 1913 lived up wonderfully to the conception which existed in the minds of Colonial families of our class; it was to us the high altar of that sacred edifice, the British Empire. Everything English was to us perfect and quite irreproachable, and though no one in our family had been born there for almost two hundred years, we still called it Home, and spoke of it with a reverence that seems now in retrospect faintly ridiculous. Ridiculous, because the English showed no gratitude, rather a contempt for this exaggerated attitude of respect. Being English, they were simple and kind-hearted, but ignorant of their own history, of what we had suffered on their account, what we had won for them and held for them on the fringes of the world. But we did not mind this neglect. On the contrary we played the sedulous ape, always ten or twenty years out of date, keeping family crests on our notepaper long after they had been dropped from the notepaper of families in England; our grandmothers wearing little white caps like Queen Victoria ten years after that monarch had been laid to rest; our sons, at great expense, being sent to schools in Australia and Africa based on English models instead of being made to avail themselves of the free education offered by the Colonies. Honeymoons were spent in England, suits and shoes were ordered from bespoke outfitters visited perhaps twenty years before. English slang was fostered and preserved often ludicrously out of date. We modelled ourselves on England and the English, but could not always prevent our native twang or accent from overlarding our speech; and coming at last by good fortune, as we were now doing, to live in England, our reward for two centuries of such loyalty might be a condescending nod from some of the local ladies who themselves had never been a hundred miles from home, and broad-bottomed, stout-legged, sure of themselves, sat in garden chairs in England, indulging in that light irony which amused them, but made us uncomfortable.

'He is a very brown little boy,' said Mrs. Bless with a laugh, when my father and mother walked back with her from church. 'Is that the African sun?'

If Mrs. Bless hoped to make my father blush, she was disappointed. My father, adoring England like his ancestors, was nevertheless very touchy about his family.

'It can't be liver at his age. It must have been the sun.'

'He has quite a nice accent, Gordon,' said Mrs. Rees-Davis, who had played golf with my father while my mother returned to fetch us. 'He might almost be taken for a little Englishman. How did you avoid that ghastly Australian twang?'

I always knew when my father was going pink with suppressed anger. A prickly sensation at the back of my neck warned me of his impending storms.

'Yer mean to sy,' he said, 'my boy talks like a pommy? After all I've sacrificed? Blow me, back he goes. First boat, see?'

Thus we fought off the first assaults. But I suppose that the English like character, and detest servility. My mother was so attractive, and my father was elegant; the only flaw was his skew-eye, the result of the train accident. I suppose that society was not very exciting in the little town of Berkhamsted to which we had come because Godfrey Huggins's family lived there, and my father had stayed with them for the three months my mother had been away collecting us and disposing of the house in Salisbury. They were showered with invitations. It seemed to me that night after night when they came to kiss us good-night, they were dressed to go out to dinner, or were hastening downstairs to receive guests. They were always in a hurry to be gone; a delicious scent, a rustle of silks, the smell of my father's shaving lotion, these remained in the ear and in the mind long after they had left the room.

There were two schools there, a boys' school which like many of the famous schools of England was an ancient foundation of the time of Henry VI, but had quite lately, under an energetic head, Dean Fry, promoted itself into a public school; and a girls' school of more recent foundation which had a fine reputation. Martin Huggins and his brothers and sisters had attended these schools, and my sisters and Clive and I were entered at them.

My father had taken a large house called Braeside, the garden of which extended from King's Road to Doctors Commons Road. When we arrived on a grey evening in June, three servants stood at the door to greet us, two of them in starched aprons and caps, the third, the gardener, in a green baize apron. This little ceremony of welcome impressed us all mightily. But if a flag had been run up from the attic floor, and if a trumpet had sounded from the upper hall, we would not have been surprised. This was England.

We had entered a new world, but one which was old and familiar, too, from the books we had all read, from anecdote and legend, from stories handed down generation after generation until the smallest amongst us had heard them and wondered at them, and now were suddenly thrust face to face with the source of them, and were awe-struck at the occasion.

My father had every reason to be distracted with his private worries, but he succumbed, as much as we did, to the atmosphere, and he took us off to the Monument and the Tower of London, to the British Museum and the Mansion House, to Madame Tussaud's and the theatre, to Soho restaurants and to Richmond and Greenwich.

He took us on visits to distant cousins in Somerset, Devon and Sussex, where we were very well received but so continuously reprimanded and admonished that we were glad to get home again. My family kept up the old habit of calling each other 'Cousin', even when that relationship was in the third or fourth degree. It seemed to me strange to be made to call an old gentleman with a white beard Cousin Horatio, and a dear old lady sitting with her canaries in the drawing-room Cousin Mary.

Money had always flowed through my father's fingers, but suddenly, at the most inappropriate moment in his career, he was extravagant even beyond his usual measure. Mr. Park, who operated the local livery, was out at all hours of the day and night, taking us to trains, meeting us at the station late at night when we returned from London, driving my parents to dinner-parties, taking us on Saturday and Sunday trips to see the surrounding countryside; Mr. Park, with his carriage and pair for formal occasions, his fly for station work, must have thought he had discovered a Colonial millionaire. But he had discovered only a Colonial family, with no income but with extravagant tastes, in that ecstasy of recognition which it experiences on finding itself at last on the sacred island.

It looked as though it should last for ever, in the estimation of a boy of eleven lately come through an experience of loneliness and deprivation. That it came quickly to an end was a shock to a mind then still without the bone of defence that comes with age and experience of life, and covers the sensitive sponge of the brain so that it can survive the incessant shocks that life provides.

My mother had developed a small lump on her left breast. Soon after we arrived in England, this was diagnosed as cancer, and it was decided that she should have an operation. This was to be done at home. Two nurses were installed; my father, ousted from my mother's room and even from his dressing-room, came to sleep with me, to my great joy.

My mother survived the operation, but was a long time mending, and in those golden September days just before school began, in a kind of weather we had never experienced before, she sat in a cane deck-chair in the garden, wrapped in rugs, looking more beautiful in my eyes than ever. I sat by the hour near her, talking to her, or sometimes just looking at her. I saw her with new eyes, the eyes of a boy of eleven, whereas the sight I had had of her before had been an infant's milky,

adoring gaze. But now I saw her with the eyes of love.
I wanted to touch her and kiss her; I longed to throw
my arms about her and crush her to me. Her life was
running out; mine was running in.

When I began school, I was put into the junior
school. I was a Day-Boy, a form of life considered by
the Boarders to be only just above the Train-Boys who
came from near-by towns by train every day. There
were five hundred boys in the school, four hundred and
ninety-nine of whom for the first few weeks I regarded
as hostile to me. The sole exception was a lanky boy,
very hirsute and ill-favoured, whose looks I discovered
hid a heart of gold. He showed me on my first day
where to hang my hat before we went into prayers in
Dean's Hall. He sat beside me and offered at the end
of the day to walk home with me. His voice, his way
of walking, his general moistness, kept impinging on
the image I had of him as the nicest and kindest boy I
had ever known, and I kept brushing these disturbing
impressions away. When we parted company on the
way home, I asked him to tea the following Sunday.
He said, 'Ow, thank you orfully,' and I said, 'Goodbye,
Alfred,' for that he had told me was his name, and had
pressed me to use it. 'Ta-ta,' he said, 'see yer tomorrow,
eh, at that old place,' and giggled, and so did I; and
then rushed home to tell my father and mother what a
splendid friend I had made and to tell them of the
pleasure they would have in meeting him next Sunday.
    'What's his name?' asked my father, smiling at this
breathless account.

'Alfred.'

'Alfred what?'

'Park.'

'Good God,' exclaimed my father, 'not Park, the liveryman's son? It must be. His father told me that his boy had won a scholarship to the school. Why out of five hundred boys do you have to pick the liveryman's son, and ask him home to tea?'

My mother soared to my defence. The debate mounted above my head. My mother asked what did it matter if he was a kind and nice boy, and had behaved so charmingly to me. She declared she would like to meet him. My father was emphatic that it was impossible. Such things couldn't be. I would have to present an excuse, say that we were going to be away for the day. Say what you damn well like, said my father, getting characteristically choleric at the end, but I simply could not have this boy to the house, and one of the first lessons I would have to learn would be to pick friends from among my own class.

This was something new; this was another shock. I had never heard of classes, but I knew what my father meant by talking of our class. He meant boys who were the sons of men like him. But that meant those boys who had looked at me with such contempt at school. How could I make friends with any of them? They openly despised me. Was I to remain friendless throughout life? I knew now what Ishmael felt in the Bible. Every man's hand was against me, too.

It was not as bad as that. My father's judgment was always right for me, and I disposed of Alfred Park next day in perfidious and despicable fashion, and to cover a sense of guilt cut him dead from that moment on.

There is nothing quite as cruel in the jungle or in the ocean as a little boy at an English school. I rapidly perfected myself in the art of being a bully to those whom everyone despised, and of adulating those whom everyone admired, thus becoming an acceptable member of the herd. I was helped in this by the discovery that I could do most things a little better than most boys, but not well enough to excite the envy of those who did not do them quite so well, or to raise myself to the pinnacle where I would have to compete with those who were really good at work or games. Without too much effort, I could hold about third place in my form, and without any experience of those games, I found I could play football and cricket well enough to merit acceptance and avoid contempt. Hostility disappeared, and after a little the ice melted, and I found myself making friends. There were even moments which I enjoyed when a feeling of physical exuberance on the playing-fields, or a flash of delight in the mind at some discovery in the classroom, made me think that this wasn't so bad after all. But those moments of afflatus were rare; on the whole I hated this time, and longed for the far-off day when my schooldays would be over.

My father's affairs did not prosper. At the end of a year we moved to a smaller house on the outskirts of Berkhamsted, though a delectable one with a wonderful orchard where I first learnt the music of English birds.

But we had not been there a month before there burst in on this music a sound of a different kind, the shrill, tense, straining sound of war. August 4, 1914, must have sounded the death-knell of my father's hopes. In a world at war there was no place for a Consulting Mining Engineer. What capital he had had nearly run out. He had taken an office in Broad Street in the City of London, and thither he went every day. But few clients consulted him; everyone's thoughts were on the war. While the drive to recruit Kitchener's Army was on, and recruiting sergeants sometimes bellowed in the street just below his window, he had to wonder in what way he could recruit his resources. I know it irked him to have to go round and see the leading men in the industry so soon after striking out on his own, and enquire about the prospects of employment. But with the expenses of my mother's illness, and four children at school, he could not stand on pride, though he must have hated to confess failure. He would talk to my mother about these things in my presence. He ignored me, and she did, too; perhaps they thought I did not understand. But I did. What I did not comprehend was the extent of the disaster. I thought it meant that there would be no bread to eat at the next meal.

My father's worries brought him and me closer together. He could not spend all his time at an office to which clients never came. He had the excuse of my mother's illness to absent himself. He would spend long hours in his study typing an article he was writing, at the suggestion of Sir Thomas Rose, the Master of the Royal Mint, on a plan for the establishment of a Mint in South Africa, but he would emerge at last, longing for exercise, and collar me, and away we would go striding over Berkhamsted Common.

To capture my interest, and make the walk enter-

F

taining for me, he invented games. There was the spelling game. He proffered the word. If I got it right, I received a halfpenny. If I got it wrong, and had some halfpennies of capital stored for words I had already spelt right, I returned one to him. When I was out of capital, I got a backward swipe of his cane at my legs. Out of capital, and two successive words wrong meant two sharp hits of the cane. It was an exciting game, and a rewarding one, for it taught me words I had at the most only a visual acquaintance with, and to spell off a run of bad luck I would sometimes ask to have examples of the use of such words, and this led to some interesting digressions.

Another game was to observe colours on a walk, in the sky, in the woods, on the clothes of people we chanced to meet, and to see who could collect the most.

Then my father, interested in his own experiment of writing the report for the Royal Mint, got me to write essays. We would discuss the subjects on the walk, and when we reached home we would take our tea to his study, and sit each side of his big desk. He would tap out his report, and I would sit and watch him covertly, thinking what a wonderful man he was, and how lucky I was to own him, and after such momentary waves of affection, bend to my task. Because I loved him I longed to please him, and because he loved words I learnt to love them and grew to hear and recognize the music they can make, and to try with an inexperienced hand to make my own combination of them sound pleasantly. This practice, begun in this simple way, was to become a habit, and was later to keep me well-fed when I might, without it, have suffered the pang of not ever having quite enough to eat.

My father was the dominant member of our family, and we all, including my mother, took our impression of life from him. When he was gay, we bathed in the radiance of his happiness; when he was melancholy, we were all subdued. He was aware of this, and did not like it, but he could not help himself or us. He came of a family in which the men were always the centre of attention, and although he was never overbearing in his manner, he was supremely selfish and he took it for granted that what suited him would suit everyone else too. The combined opposition of the Cunningham family had not been able to deter him from marrying my mother, and when he had carried her off he accepted it as quite natural that she should give up her faith and adopt his. She could not have done this without a prolonged and agonizing period of indecision, and the fact that we were all as children sent to convents showed that she had not given in without a struggle. But in the end she surrendered as we all did to his overpowering will.

He had a charming character, and was liked by men as well as women. He was very extravagant in his tastes, and even when his money ran out, as it did in the first years of the first World War, he continued to buy his suits at Poole's in Savile Row, and to remain a member of his various clubs. When we were at our lowest ebb of poverty, and sometimes were hungry, the scent of his after-dinner cigar would be a reminder in the house that Father, deep in melancholy for the moment at some fresh and threatening turn in his fortunes, was with us physically, if not visibly, for on such evenings he would shut himself in his study with orders that he was not to be disturbed. We crept like unhappy ghosts up and down the stairs, making our way to bed or to the play-room, hushed by my mother who looked increasingly sad and worn.

I thought she was sad because we had become poor, but time makes clear the pattern which our lives have made, and what we were then too young to recognize becomes clearer in the perspective which age offers of our youth.

The old jealousy returned. Soon after the war broke out, Mike Drummond came from South Africa to join the army. He enlisted in the Black Watch, and soon afterwards was given a commission. By the spring of 1915, just as we were running upon our first hard times, and my mother was recovering from her operation, he went to France. He had come often to stay with us while he was training in England, and, older now, and with an acuter ear, I caught in the tone of his voice and in my mother's that same sound of secret understanding which had ravaged me and made me unhappy in Africa. He came home on leave from France two or three times in the next two years. By then he had risen to the rank of major, and had been decorated. He brought with him on leave a German helmet, and souvenirs of the muddy world he had left. He was heroic in size and in the splendour of his uniform and tartan trews, and my father was out of work and sunk in despair. He came like a great gale of heroism into the melancholy atmosphere of our home, and while he was there my father's will ceased to impose itself in the house, and my mother's anxiety disappeared. We were showered with presents and rich foods. My father seemed to retreat more into his study, and I crept in there with him, nursing my jealousy and longing to comfort him. He said I was spending too much time indoors, and I knew that he wanted to be alone, but I clung to him and to my writing, until Mike went back to France, and I could leave him alone again.

We had moved to a still smaller house in Berkhamsted, our third in just over two years, when financial relief finally came. Sir Thomas Rose offered my father the post of Metallurgist at the Royal Mint in Ottawa. It was not a very grand job, but it was better than nothing. My mother's health having temporarily improved, it was decided that we should be left at school in England, that she should remain here to keep a home for us in the holidays, and that my father should take with him my younger sister, Rene, who had just finished school, both for company and so that she might find a job in Canada.

There cannot have been another time in the history of England like those years, 1914 to 1918, when English youth fell in France and Belgium. A gateway gave onto the school grounds at Berkhamsted. Once you entered there, you found yourself on a gravelled broadwalk, and facing a square of buildings which ran round the grass plot called the Quad. To the left stood the library and school house, the ancient buildings which were the original foundation. To the right were the school chapel and cloisters, of fairly recent nineteenth-century design. These were joined to the chemistry building, called inevitably 'Stinks', and this portent of the new age joined at right angles Dean's Hall, the sanctum where the whole school met for roll-call and prayers every morning. This side of the quadrilateral was formed by the junior school, and the remaining side, at right angles to it, was a conglomeration of buildings which included the school swimming-bath, the fives courts, the tuck-shop, and a space in which stood an ancient oak tree of enormous dimensions, slashed and scarred by the aspiring penknives of generations of boys, and surrounded by a wooden seat.

This was the little world, the quadrilateral, in which I spent those four years while the youth of Europe was being slain in muddy fields a hundred miles away. Day by day the headmaster would read out at morning prayers the names of Old Boys who had fallen in action since the previous day's list. Black-bordered cards, with the Old Boy's name, the years he was at the school, the regiment with which he was serving, the battle in which he had fallen, were affixed to the walls of the cloisters. At first a dozen or twenty names, at which we gazed in solemn admiration; then with the holocaust of Loos and the Somme a veritable snow-storm of cards, until in 1917 the long wall of the cloisters was filled from top to bottom with these black-bordered cards, each representing a life that had flowered in this quadrilateral of ugly red buildings. By 1917 we hardly glanced at them as we milled down the cloisters to our classrooms.

And yet, in my occasional nightmares, this roll of the dead would reappear. I could feel myself being sucked into the vortex. There were three years yet before I could be called to go, but time was vanishing, and death was advancing on me. My father, chief prop of my life, had gone away, and my mother, I realized suddenly in the spring of 1917 with a feeling of panic, was dying.

For a long time her dry cough had sounded through the house all day; she moved like a ghost, silent and pale, about us. Coming downstairs on a morning in the Easter holidays, I found her in a faint lying on the dining-room floor. We had then no servants in the house; she had got up early and had evidently been clearing the dining-room fire when she lost consciousness.

It was the most frightening moment of my life to see her lying there on the floor, pale as death. I did not run for the others, but flew to her, raised her head upon my knees and kissed her and rubbed her temples furiously with my cold hands. Whether it was this vigorous treatment that revived her I do not know, but her eyelids fluttered open. I saw in the deep still blue of her eyes the light come like a lantern carried very far away; then swiftly she recognized me, sighed and said, 'Oh, Rache!'

With no other word between us, I helped her up to her room, and while she undressed hurried down to make her a cup of tea. When I came upstairs again she was in bed. I put the tray down, sat on her bed, and took her hand, and waited trembling for her to confirm my fear that she was about to die.

She smiled at me, and pretended to take it lightly. 'Don't look so worried, Rache, you frighten me.'

But when she saw I didn't respond to this, she quickly became serious.

'You mustn't tell Father, or the others, anything about this. Promise me that, won't you? The doctor says I have a bad lung and must rest a great deal. You know how impossible that is without any help in the house. But I have promised to take things as quietly as possible. I shouldn't have tried to do that fire before I had had breakfast. But you must promise me that you will not say anything to anyone. If you do, Father will have to give up his work and come home, and we will literally be without any money at all. I'll be much better when the warm weather comes. We will go down to Worthing for our holidays and I will soon get right again.'

I promised, but it was a promise that I could not wait to break. Later that afternoon, when my mother was resting, I wrote to my father and told him exactly what had happened. I told him of the promise that she had extracted from me, and I asked him earnestly not to show that I had broken it, but to get us all out to Canada as quickly as possible.

It took six months to arrange. The submarine attack on England was at its worst in that summer of 1917, and passages for so large a party, requiring three cabins, were not easy to arrange. But at last in September we were warned to be ready. We came up from Berkhamsted and stayed at Brown's Hotel. One morning early in the middle of that month we left for Liverpool, boarded the *Metagama*, joined a convoy, and started on the grim voyage across the North Atlantic.

CHAPTER FOUR

BY this time my mother was desperately ill, and the slow zigzagging path we swept across the grey ocean was agonizingly slow. I knew that at any moment we might be torpedoed and that I might find myself helpless in those heaving, angry, cold seas. I thought about my mother, but I thought of myself too, and of what a great loss it would be if my life were to be stifled out of me at the age of fifteen in this heaving ocean. It was not fear of death that anguished me as I stood on the deck of that rolling ship with my lifebelt on my shoulders; it was the thought of the loss of all the years ahead. I did not think of the pleasures that I would miss, but of the feats that I would never achieve. I did not know then what life would make of me, or of what kind these achievements would be; I only knew that if I were given the opportunity, I could do something with my life, and it was the thought of being cheated out of that opportunity that made those slow hours pass so agonizingly, and made me hate myself for thinking these thoughts when I should have been thinking of my mother lying helpless and ill below decks.

There came a morning when, waking in my berth, which was an inside one, I heard through the port-hole in the gangway the sound of sea-birds and with a sudden rush of relief realized that the ship was not behaving in the way that it had done for twelve days but was moving steadily on its course, neither zig-zagging as it had done all across the ocean, nor rising to meet the hissing waves and falling into the troughs beyond. My God, I thought, we have survived it. I dressed quickly and rushed up on deck, barely pausing to look at my mother in her cabin. There was no land in sight and, for a moment, I felt dismayed; but within a minute or two I realized that the smell of land was there. We were on the Grand Banks off Newfoundland. Sea-birds soared and dipped over the ship; a grey mist hung like a curtain before us and the ship moved steadily on and a feeling of land and of safety grew, until I felt an excitement dancing in my blood and I smiled and talked to people whom, with the shyness characteristic of my age, I had avoided all through the voyage.

We reached Montreal at night, and I saw for the first time in my life, for I had always lived in the country and had known London only in war-time, a city blazing with light. My mother remained in her cabin, but I waited with my elder sister and my brother on deck until my father came striding up the gangway, kissed us all and hurried below to my mother's cabin. We all felt an immense relief now that he had taken over.

But my mother had come to Canada only to die. She lived three weeks after that night. She was un-conscious much of the last week. But in the time before that, when she could be brought to the balcony of the little apartment to sit at midday in the strong autumn sunshine for an hour or two, staring at this strange vividly coloured Canadian scene, she must have felt as lonely as a bird in a cage. She had come a long way from the happy scenes of her childhood, and she told me that it frightened her to think that her body would soon be put for ever in the cold ground of a country in which she had known no friends.

The apartment was so small, and the crisis in it so grave, that Clive and I were continually being sent out for walks. Day after day we explored the banks of the three rivers, the Ottawa, the Rideau and the Gatineau, that meet spectacularly below the cliffs on which the Canadian Houses of Parliament stand. Everything was on such a majestic scale, these roaring rivers compared with the slow-moving Grand Junction Canal near which we had lived for years, this great bowl of clear-cut blue sky compared with the tender misty one that had covered us in England; this pungent, overpowering smell of dying Nature compared with the faint, half-rotten odour, compounded of smoke and beech-leaves and damp ground, which marks the same season in England. Even the horses we saw in the fields seemed nearly twice the size of English horses.

We often talked of what we were going to do. The school year had started, and Clive should have been at school. My father and mother had mentioned several times the need of my father going to see the headmaster about entering him. Because of my age I was in a more uncertain state. It was presumed that I had finished with school. There was no university in Ottawa, but McGill in Montreal was only one hundred miles away. The academic year there had also started. Nothing could be done about this while my mother was so ill. I was glad of that. I was not yet ready to meet Canadian youth.

But from the moment a week or two before when I had come out on the deck of the *Metagama* in the bright morning and seen the Canadian land for the first time, I had been swept with a passion for it. The sensation was as sudden, as rapturous as love. This feeling might have sprung in the first place, on that still, misty morning, from relief at knowing that we were out of danger. If I had arrived at any other season than the Fall, I might have felt less intoxicated than I did. But the wonderful relief that came from the knowledge that we were safe at last, and the indescribable beauty of these magnificent heights rising above the great river in tiers of crimson and gold to a superb sky of tremendously vivid blue, left an impression on me that was never to be eradicated.

My father reminded us that we were Canadian by origin, and that his father had been the first in the family to leave Canada and settle elsewhere, and it thrilled me to think that it was to this beautiful land that my ancestors had come one hundred and sixty years before. It sent a shiver over my skin to think of those hardy pioneers, moving on their slow ponderous way through the wilderness, pushing back the French, the makers of routes, the *coureurs du bois* who, through the blind forests and along intricate waterways, had established missions and stations as far as the Gulf of Mexico. Yes, it thrilled me, ultimate link in this long chain that had been turned through the centuries, and had persevered over all obstacles which by its endurance and strength enabled me now to stand at this confluence of rivers, and to think of these races contending for a continent which then lay untouched in all its primitive power and promise; where I now stood, and around me, behind me, the interminable forests, the vast lakes, the majestic rivers flowing north, east, south and west. And over it all brooding the tremendous silence of the primitive world, broken then only as a striking clock breaks the silence of a room at night, by the cry of an animal, the sound of an avalanche, the breaking of a bough under its weight of snow, the thunder of a cataract somewhere in the hills. It was thrilling for me to stand there at fifteen in Canada and realize all that.

Clive and I talked a great deal of these things in our long walks. At least I did the talking, and he as always was the patient, flattering listener. I swore to Clive that I would go no more to school or university, that I would make my own life as a farmer here, and that when he finished school he could join me.

One day on a walk we saw a painted board which said DOMINION EXPERIMENTAL FARM, and a painted finger which pointed to DAIRY. 'Let's go and look,' I said to Clive, and we followed the narrow path that led to some corrugated iron buildings a few hundred yards away.

'I'm going to see if they'll give me a job,' I said on a sudden impulse. 'You wait here.'

Obediently he stood, while I walked forward to a door which led into one of the buildings at the end of the path. There was nothing to show that it was private. I gave a fumbled knock and pushed it open gently. From inside came a smell of warm, sweet animal flesh, and the hum of machinery. Both beckoned me on. Somebody called out, 'Shut that door!' I closed it behind me, and looked out over a sea of cows' backs to the other side of the building, 150 feet away.

I had never seen anything like it. I did not know

that so many animals could be packed into a single building. There must have been over a thousand head of cattle standing there in orderly rows as neat and almost as quiet as a regiment of Guards at Trooping the Colours. The hour was about four o'clock in the afternoon and I had arrived at the time of milking. The sweet, low, throaty sounds that cows make when they are being relieved of the pressure on their bags, and at the same time are eating wisps of hay, echoed in the high building. The hum I had heard came from the milking machines which were in use up and down the lines. There must have been fifty cows in each line facing head to head, and there must have been twenty lines altogether. They were divided according to breed: the brown-and-white Friesian cows, the black-and-white Holsteins, and the pigmy black cows that were a native French-Canadian breed. They were separated from each other by a low wall on which hung a chart which I later learnt gave each one's daily milk yield, the butter and fat content, and marked the times of their calving. There were a dozen white-coated attendants in the room who moved swiftly and silently from animal to animal, fastening the long rubber teats on the udder of one cow, washing off the bag of another, finishing a third by hand, entering up the data on the chart of still another. The only sound was the low hum of the electric motor working the milkers, the muted vibration of animal sound from the contented cows, and the occasional clatter as a full milk-churn was rolled on its base up to the concrete platform where I stood, which was three feet or more above the level on which the cows were placed.

'Looking for someone, son?' asked one of these

men as he rolled a forty-gallon milk-churn near to me.

'I want to see the manager.'

'Andy Curwen? He'll be in the office. Along there to the right.'

I made my way along the platform about twenty yards and there was a boarded-in section, painted green, with glass windows giving on the barn. I could see a naked bulb beneath a white shade, a slanting desk, and a thin man with a bald head leaning against it and writing. I knocked timidly at the door, heard no summons, knocked again, and after a moment's anxious pause pushed the door open slowly. I could hear a sibilant whisper, nothing more; it was exactly as though someone was passing some secret information, and I had stumbled upon him in the act.

But Mr. Curwen did not turn from the desk, and I saw that it was he who was doing the whispering. He was adding under his breath. Now that I stood still and listened, I could hear him totting up the numbers, and see his poised pencil make its way down some column. Then there was an audible smacking of the lips and a total figure was evidently subscribed. The pencil was thrown down with a clatter and he turned to face me.

'Well, young feller?' he enquired. He was thin beyond imagining, a man like a fresh shaving of wood peeled from some timber, as pale, as clean, as threadbare. He wore gold-rimmed spectacles, he had a thin pink face with clear blue eyes, a corrugated forehead which rose to a shiny bald skull, and he wore a pair of overalls which had been so frequently and thoroughly washed that they were now practically the colour of the sky they must so often have stretched out under while they were being dried.

'Well, young feller?'

I was terribly nervous. This was the first time I had ever asked for a job. He might send me packing, he might laugh at me scornfully, he might curse and revile me for wasting his time : I hadn't the faintest notion of what was coming to me, and I was so nervous I could hardly speak.

'I want a job,' I said, and swallowed quickly to relieve my dry throat. 'I want to know if I can work here.'

He did none of the things I had expected. He looked at me thoughtfully, swinging his long thin legs each side of the stool.

'So you want a job, eh ? Just walk in like that and ask for it, and expect to get it, eh? You don't look to me as if you'd ever done much work. How old are you ?'

I was about to reply sixteen, when I suddenly thought that might get me into trouble.

'Seventeen,' I replied.

'When did you leave school ?'

'Two months ago.'

'English, ain't yer ?'

'Yes.'

'Where's your family ?'

'In . . . in Ottawa.'

'They know you're out here asking for a job ? Know the kind of hours we keep here, son ? 5.30 A.M. to 5.30 P.M., twelve hours a day sure, six days a week, too, and Sunday shift by rotation. You look kind of undeveloped to me. I don't figure you could get up at 4.30, say, in your city apartment, and be out here, breakfasted and ready to work, by 5.30, not with your parents' consent.'

'My parents won't mind. That is to say, my mother's very ill, and everyone thinks it's better if my brother and I are out of the house all day. My brother will be going to school, but I mean to get a job.'

'You do, eh, darn yer.' He gave a little cackle of laughter. 'You go home and see yer Pa, and tell him you want to work here. Say Andy Curwen said, why sure, you could have a job, fifteen cents an hour, twelve hours a day. See what yer Pa says. O.K., if he'll let you, why you're as good as signed on. And if I don't see you again, I'll know he's designing you for something better.'

He swung round on his stool, picked up his pencil and tackled another column of figures. When I said, 'Goodbye, Mr. Curwen,' the whisper swelled into harsh speech to shut out my interruption and protect the process of addition. I closed the door softly behind me, and almost ran along the platform, bursting open the door at the end, and waving to Clive, who still stood where I had left him.

'I've got a job,' I said, seizing his arm. 'I'm going to work here.'

I told him what Mr. Curwen had said about asking Father.

'Perhaps he won't let you,' said Clive.

'He'll let me all right,' I said. 'Don't you see, we get on his nerves hanging about. We remind him that he should be doing something about us. With me away, he'll be able to fix you up at school, and then he'll have only Mother to worry about.'

*

G

My father did not mind. In fact he seemed quite proud of my exploit. The others all showed a momentary interest in the fact that I was about to start my working life, but I didn't remain the centre of attention for very long.

The next morning I walked out to the Experimental Farm and told Mr. Curwen that my father was agreeable to my starting work. I was signed on, and he told me to get myself a pair of overalls and some stout boots and to be there the next morning at 5.30. He asked me if I had a bicycle, and I said 'No.'

'There won't be any street-cars running. How you going to make it?'

I said I'd walk, and he looked at me curiously for a moment and then burst into a cackle of laughter.

'O.K.,' he said, 'you walk. Come and see me in the office as soon as you get here.'

My father advanced me five dollars to buy the overalls, a lunch-pail and an alarm clock. I did not dare to mention the extravagance of a bicycle, and it did not seem to have occurred to him how I was going to get to my job. I set the alarm for four o'clock, and awoke in the terrible blackness of the night to its shrill summons. Clive and I were still sharing a room: this was before my father had left my mother's room in the last stage of her illness. Clive stirred uneasily in his sleep but did not waken. I dragged myself out of bed shivering and feeling quite sick with fatigue and sudden fright, turned on the light and started to pull on my clothes.

When I was dressed I had to tiptoe to the kitchen to get my breakfast, and when I had made some coffee and boiled an egg, I had to make jam sandwiches for my lunch. Then I went down the back wooden stairs to the street and started the walk to the Experimental Farm three miles away.

I was frightened of the dark. I had been for years, ever since the experience in Salisbury. I was alone in the streets. From the darkness behind each house I dreaded what might appear. I walked alone in the centre of the road, feeling the night air cold on my face and against my chest, but not cold enough to keep my skin from burning with tension.

It was a relief to come to the farm and to see the lights in the buildings, and a physical pleasure to come into the barns where the warm breath of the animals rose like steam towards the girders of the roof and the smell of hay was fresh and tickling to the nose.

My job at first was the humble one of scraping away the droppings of the night. This I did with a hoe-like instrument, pulling them to the edge of the byre where they fell into a channel, then sweeping them along to the end, shovel the heap into a barrow and wheel it away. It wasn't a very romantic task, and undertaken twice a day, when I first came and before I went home, it took a couple of hours and was really the main part of my activity. The rest of the time I cleaned the animals, fetched fodder from the silo, put hay in the racks, hosed out the milk-churns and occasionally helped Mr. Curwen in the office with his forms. At the end of the day I had my journey home, and at the end of a 72-hour week, not including seven hours spent walking to work, I had ten dollars and eighty cents. And I was mightily tired. So tired that on the seventh day I could hardly rise from bed at all; so tired each night when I got home that after washing myself and changing for supper, and after talking to my mother for a little, I could not stay up but was in bed even before Clive was, an indignity which I could never have supported had I not been worn beyond endurance.

I had never known what it was to be laughed at and ridiculed before, and I found it difficult to submit, but there was no alternative. Mr. Curwen seemed to regard me as a freak, and there was no doubt that I caused him great amusement. He had a way of asking apparently simple questions and then bursting into a cackle of laughter, turning his back on me as he did so. I found it intolerable, but I would not have risked losing my job by calling him to account.

The other men in the dairy numbered about seven. They stared at me on the first morning as though there was something peculiar about me. They kept up amongst themselves a continuous bantering talk. When the break for lunch came, they all went up to the end of the barn where the hay came down from a chute, and made themselves comfortable on the half-ton of hay that lay always spread loosely on the floor. I followed them timidly with my lunch-pail, and sat on the extreme outside of their circle, eating my jam sandwiches. I noticed that the other men, who had wives, I supposed, to prepare their lunches, had a variety of things in their lunch-pails, like hard-boiled eggs and cheese and apples, and I was ashamed of my badly-cut and rather soggy heap of jam sandwiches.

I listened to their talk and did not find it edifying. I was young, and solemn, and cold, and not a little tired,

and I was sorry for myself, and my little scraps of food
seemed to me a mark of my neglect and poverty. So I
turned my back on the chatter and shivered and ate,
and then lay full length on the hay, as the others did;
but unlike them, fell asleep.

The afternoons seemed endless. I first learned in
that great barn to hate idleness. There was a pause in
the day's activities at about 2.30 when there was literally
nothing to do until the milking began and my own
menial task of scraping the cement floor clear of manure
commenced at about 4 P.M. Never did the hours pass
so slowly as those, when the men smoked cigarettes
to pass the time and I wandered up and down reading
the records of milk yields and butter-fat content and
calvings past and anticipated. A sort of gloomy-
cold silence descended on the barn at that hour, and
my spirits were at their lowest. It was then that I
thought of my mother, wondering whether she had
suffered much during the day. I now knew that she
was dying, though I had no idea how close the final
moment was. But in those late afternoons, standing
about idle, when the cold came to smite me, and my thin
young stomach growled angrily for hot food, I touched
depths of depression I have never known since, because
I have never since been both hungry and cold day after
day. In that state of melancholy and self-pity, turning
from reading the graphs of a cow's career, and seeing
her velvet eyes turned in liquid enquiry upon me, asking
I suppose whether I had come to relieve her of her milk
— it was not surprising that I should put my arms over
the warm back of the cow and touch her large velvet
ears for the sake of their exquisite softness and warmth.

On the afternoon of October 21st, the first snow

came. It had been bitterly cold for the two days previously. Gone were the deep-blue skies of the Fall, and the crimson and gold leaves had been blown from the trees in the icy wind which snarled and bit at us, and brought heavy grey clouds to cover the sky. I thought of my walk home, not so long as in the mornings because in the evenings I could get a street-car only a mile from the Experimental Farm which took me within a block of home. But I thought ahead to the following morning, and wondered, if the snow continued to fall all night, how I could possibly walk to work in the morning.

I ran up the back stairs at home, an outside staircase used only by the delivery men and the garbage collectors, but used by me going to and coming from work. It led straight onto the kitchen. I stamped my feet heavily coming up the stairs to remove the wet snow which was caked on the soles of my nailed boots. My father put his head through the door and placed a finger to his lips. I thought he meant to remind me that my mother was sleeping, but when I came into the kitchen I saw that a difference had come over him, and I knew at once that the moment we had all been dreading was at hand.

'The doctor has just been. He says Mother will not last throughout the night. She is under drugs and sleeping. Don't go in to her now.'

He did not stay to talk to me, but went away with stricken face, and I heard him shut the door to the study which for the last few nights he and I had been sharing as a bedroom. I took off my boots in the kitchen and then went to Clive's little room to take off my overalls. All was silent in the flat. I could hear the subdued murmur of my sisters' voices in the drawing-room, and

I supposed that Clive was sitting with them, for there was no sign of him here. When I had peeled off my overalls and pulled on my trousers, I tiptoed to the bathroom to wash. At the end of the hall was my mother's room. I could see a dim light burning there. I could not prevent myself — it was not curiosity, it was love — from stealing on tiptoe in my stockinged feet to my mother's door and looking at her, the last time I knew that I was to see her in life.

She was asleep. She was in that sleep that is a drifting into death, the slow, laborious parting from consciousness. She was propped up amongst innumerable pillows. She seemed to me as beautiful as she had always been: that same blue-black hair shining and parted in the centre, those same beautifully-moulded and arched eye-sockets, that delicate skin like a magnolia. Her head was turned sideways as though she looked down the brief channel of her life. I could hear her heavy breathing, and see, where her night-dress opened, what I had never seen before, the cruel scar left by her operation in 1913, the wound which after years had now led her to this death.

I had no part in the last moments which came at about two o'clock in the morning. I had not meant to go to sleep; I meant to wait until my father came. I wanted to talk to him, and to try to get that unfamiliar stricken look from his face. When he came it would be to tell me that Mother had died, and I wanted to comfort him in his unhappiness. I thought of what I could say when he made this pronouncement that would match the tremendous drama of the moment, and at the same time assure him of my undying love for him. 'She is with the angels,' I would cry, and fling my arms around his neck, and weep with him.

The long day with its toil and its burden of emotion was too much for me. I had no sooner stretched out on top of the bed than I sank into sleep; only to jerk out of it with thudding heart when the light was switched on, and my father stumbled into the room. He sat down beside me on the bed and put his hand on my forehead. 'She has gone, old son. It is all over.'

I did what I had foreseen doing, and said what I had thought to say, and for a few moments, the first since I had been a child, we abandoned ourselves to grief and to the love we each had for the other, but which we had taught ourselves not to show. Then my father told me to go to sleep, and he bent over and kissed me; and through half-closed wet eyes I watched him prepare for bed, kneeling and saying his prayers while the light shone on his bent head, and my heart swelled and contracted painfully with love for him.

The morning broke with the wind rattling and buffeting at our windows. At six o'clock my father stirred and groaned, and came awake. I knew that he had only slept fitfully, because I had, and I had been watching him in the dark for some time.

He sat up on the edge of the bed, and seeing I was awake, he said: 'You might as well go to work, old son. It will get you out of the house. It will be miserable here.'

'But can't I help you, Dad ? Can't I stay with you ?'

'No, you go along. I'll attend to everything. There's a good chap.'

I did not know how to put it to him that I was embarrassed to go to work. I would have to say why I was late. I would have to say that my mother had died in the night. They would be shocked that I had come, as though I were greedy for my wage. I couldn't explain this to my father, and I could not lie and say that it was because I didn't want to leave Mother. She was dead ; she had become a stranger. From that corpse, so still and so unnaturally resembling her, indeed I wanted to get away.

So I struggled into my working clothes, and ate some bread and drank some coffee standing up in the little kitchen, looked at my lunch-pail and thought, hell, I couldn't eat my lunch even if it was there, and without a further word to anyone ran down the back steps and made my way to the street-car. When I reached the farm, I went straight to Andy's office. It was warm in there, and cheerful and alive and light. He swung round on his stool :

'Well, young feller, been out all night raising hell, I bet, chasing the girls, and slept in, I guess ?'

'No, Mr. Curwen, I . . . My mother, well, she died in the night, last night.'

His forehead went up into its familiar, corrugated frown, his bald head sliding down to meet it. Then he slipped off his stool.

'Jeez, kid, I'm sorry. What are you doing here then ? Why did you come out ? Whyn' you just phone ?'

'My father thought I might as well come to work.'

That sounded terrible. 'I mean, he thought I'd be better out of the way.'

Andy Curwen grew excited, the way he did when he was trying to make people see sense.

'You go right home, kid. No matter what your father says, that's where you should be. What the hell, we got to think of ourselves, don't we? Fine bunch of slave-drivers we would look, you doing a day's work here today. God-damn it, I won't have it. You get right home, and don't come back here until after the funeral.'

He hissed through his teeth in the way that I knew, turned his back on me and drummed with his fingers impatiently on the desk, sure sign that he was upset. I loved him in that minute. I did not want to work, I wanted to be with my father. I wanted to be doing something on this unusual day, but I needed a reason to go home, and Andy Curwen's order had given it to me.

'Thank you, Mr. Curwen.'

He turned and looked at me.

'You all right for money, son?'

'Sure, I'm all right.'

He opened his old-fashioned purse and took out a five-dollar bill. 'Here, this will help. Don't want to ask your Dad at a time like this. Keep it just in case. Go on now, git going.' He turned back impatiently to his desk.

I was home again before my father was dressed and ready to go out. I told him what had happened; Mr. Curwen said I was to go home, and not come back until after the funeral. My father said all right, I had better come along with him. I changed into my good suit, and when we were leaving the flat, he looked at me and said, 'You can't wear that hat.' He fumbled in the dark hall cupboard and drew out one of his hats, a black Homburg, and said, 'Try this.'

The hat fitted, but it felt enormous on top of my young face, and my father could not restrain a rueful smile. 'Wear it further forward on your nose, old son, you look as though it's crushing you.'

We set off in the windy morning. Oh, I was happy to be with my father. I scarcely thought of my mother. My father was suddenly gentle and considerate with me. He spoke to me warmly, and looked at me affectionately, and I responded, as I always did at any notice he took of me.

Our first call was at the bank. My father went into the manager's office, and I was left sitting in the hall, watching the curious, glittering scene, holding my black hat between my knees. After a little while the door of the manager's office opened, and there was my father saying goodbye. He called me over and introduced me. Mr. Hamilton looked at me as we talked, and then drew us back into his office, holding the door with one hand.

'Rather a sad occasion, Dickson,' he said. 'Like to leave this young fellow with me? I'll take him out and give him some lunch, and then send him home afterwards.'

' Well, old chap ?' said my father enquiringly.

'I'd better go with you,' I said. 'Thanks, though,' I added to Mr. Hamilton.

It seemed to me that there was an awkward pause of a moment, then Mr. Hamilton clapped me on the shoulder, and said: 'That's all right, my boy. Some other time we'll have that lunch. You come and see me whenever you like.'

We left the bank and walked as far as the Château Laurier. Then we caught a street-car for the cemetery. My father was very silent on the way out, and I could tell that something had happened at the bank to upset him. A thin snow that was almost like sleet dashed against the windows of the street-car. Everything looked sad; it was the beginning of winter, and I remembered what my mother had said about lying under the snow.

At the end of the line we got out and walked up the sloping road to the cemetery. I remember that it was rutty, and caked with wet, melting snow, and that boarded sidewalks lined it on each side. Suddenly there were the gates, and a stone-built lodge just inside. We had left behind the decrepit, untidy, broken-down, poverty-marked houses and streets where the living struggled for life; we were in the city of the dead. As far as the eye could see there were gravestones, and, as though an army of the sheeted dead had swept and tidied up the place before lying down to take their eternal rest, even the light fall of snow of the night before did not show. The pale grass glistened wetly and the trees bent over the graves in grief. But there was a feeling like a prison about the place. Once in here, once admissible to the ranks of the dead, you could never get out. Here was the last halt before you took the wingèd flight. I shivered, and I thought what a terrible thing it was to die. What a loneliness to be placed here, and for the living to turn their backs, and to lift their faces to the light and to life again.

My father had expressed his requirements, and plans were drawn out and unrolled. We were renting a chamber in the house of the dead. We discussed accessibility, position, prices. Oh God, it was terrible to be so matter-of-fact. My father leant across the counter as though he were ordering a suit of clothes, yet I knew by the clipped, sardonic way in which he spoke that he hated this. Afterwards, I knew, we would compare notes and observations about the man who was attending to us; his patter, appropriate to grave-dealings, I could almost hear my father say; his large full red underlip, 'Loves his food, a greedy sensual man'; his stubby fingers with dirty flat nails, 'Barely put down the spade, and he comes to serve us': the echo of these sharp, thrusting phrases before he had even spoken them assailed my inner ear and made me miserable, and my father turned to me and said, 'Wait for me outside, old chap. I won't be long.'

I stood there outside the door, looking along the silent, bare avenues. The thin sleet fell, and after a minute or two it melted from my black hat and dripped down my neck, and I pushed the hat back on my head to protect me.

My father came out, and without a word we started to walk briskly down the muddy roadway to the street-car stop. I stared straight ahead, but I could feel him glancing now and then at me. I knew that he wanted to say something to comfort me, but he could not find the words. I wanted to comfort him, but I was afraid to speak before he did. We had always been able to communicate, but never about ourselves. We both knew that the moment wasn't right to joke about Charon, whom we had left behind in the office, rolling up his plans and shutting the drawers. Then my father suddenly spoke, thrusting his arm through mine.

'You will miss your mother, old chap, more than any of the others will. She loved you best of us all.'

'Oh, Dad.'

'Only forty-two. It's young to die. A mysterious thing, to be singled out for such pain. She might have been alive today if it had not been for some accident. Years ago, perhaps when you were all babies. One of you, suckling at the breast. They know nothing about cancer. A blow, hardly noticed at the time, can make an injury out of which, years later, this horrible growth can come.'

My father went on talking while the ugly world about me grew dark and threatening. I walked on beside him, a sense of guilt beginning to well up in me. I knew that it could not be proved that I had been responsible, but I had been the loved one. I, was it I, walking along this snow-covered road, who sucking life from her with greedy lips had dealt her the fatal blow ? I knew that this uneasy feeling, like the one I had nursed after that night in Salisbury, was to stay with me and grow in me, and I stared at the wet road and the dark, ugly wooden houses that lined it on either side with frightened eyes. This was the hostile world and I now had to face it on my own.

CHAPTER FIVE

MY mother's death broke up our family; it was as though we had been held together only by her love; when that was withdrawn, our love for each other was withdrawn too. My sister Rene, who had been in Ottawa for a year and a half with my father, had made many friends: she was seventeen and very pretty, and soon she was going out every night. My elder sister, Mitta, joined Rene's friends and we saw little of her. And soon it became apparent to me that my father was restive and was only coming home at nights out of a sense of duty to be with Clive and me. He was fifty-two, slender, handsome, extremely popular, an unattached widower: invitations were pressed on him, and he couldn't decline them all. He was kind and thoughtful and at first apologetic about his evening absences, but soon Clive and I were left alone in the flat at night.

Clive had made his own friends at school. His first name was Gordon and summoning cries of 'Gawd', at the sound of which my father would flinch if he were at home, would be shouted up to our balcony in the early dusk of winter evenings. His face would break into radiance at the sound; I could not bear it and would look away. He would walk to the balcony, and I would hear the invitations to him to come to the rink at the school, and soon he would be away until nine

or nine-thirty at night, having gone to other boys'
houses for supper afterwards. I was often left alone in
the empty flat, nervous, and starting at every creak and
murmur of the house. Night after night I sat at the
dining-room table trying to write, but nothing substantial came of my efforts. All they did was to occupy
my close attention and give me the feeling of being
creative, but when the short stories or the poetry I
attempted were done, I could see that they were no
good. When I had my father alone on some evening,
or on Sunday afternoons, I would read them to him.
He criticized them constructively, and told me how to
rewrite them, but left alone on the next evening I would
have no heart for repair jobs, and would strike at something new, which in turn took its place in my mounting
pile of failed efforts. All I got from these empty
evenings was exercise in literary composition; it made
me eloquent and swift with my pen, but it did not
teach me to think before I wrote; I wrote and flattered
myself that I was thinking, but all I was doing was to
imitate what I had read. It was like playing the piano
by ear instead of reading music from sight.

But I was less tired. I had given up the farm.
When I went back after the funeral, I was unhappy and
I hated the drudgery, the cold, the ugly talk. Leaving
the flat on those winter mornings had been harder
than ever, knowing that when I returned at night it
might be empty, and as dark and deserted as when I
left it. Besides, Mr. Hamilton's face was constantly in
my mind. He had been friendly to me, even though I
had sensed on that terrible morning that there was some
antagonism between Father and him. I had not lived
through these last few years without being able to guess

what was the reason for their strained feelings. But plainly he had not included me in his area of dispute, and it was nice to be smiled on and, I daresay, to be felt sorry for.

One Saturday morning I took time off from the farm, and went to see him. I had to tell Father what I was going to do, and he as usual smiled and said, 'Go ahead, old son. You don't want to be shovelling muck all your life. See what Hamilton says.'

Once again I found myself in that brass-grilled room, warm with central heating and a smell which I associated with money. I was taken in to see Mr. Hamilton, and it was like seeing an old friend. He took me on as a bank messenger at $25 a month, and it was arranged that I should start on Monday week, when I had worked out my notice at the farm.

Twenty-five dollars a month wasn't much money, but the life was easy after the farm. I could get a hot lunch of soup with mashed potatoes in it and a cup of hot coffee at one of those cafeterias called a Bowles one-armed lunch, where you sat in a chair one arm of which broadened out into a table. This diet, which was not substantial, but which warmed my entrails, cost only 15 cents. It was better than lying on the hay and eating sandwiches from a lunch-pail. I had bought a winter overcoat for $15 and I was clean and shining and warm all day. And the work was interesting. I was working at a branch of the bank in the market district of Ottawa. My job was to collect bills, and for half the day I would be out, going from shop to shop and presenting my bills. I was fascinated with the types I met, Poles and Ukrainians running seed shops and leather shops. I began to notice the extraordinary variety of the human

H

face, and to see for the first time what it mirrored; for the first time in life, for I had seen it before in the books I had read, and could have recognized it instantly in print. The shock was to see it in life. I could imagine, and did, what deeps of feeling were hidden behind these immense, clumsy bodies, from which issued this broken, defensive, expostulative talk, flung at me, for I came to demand payment; I was retribution, the date become due. For the first time I saw the human face as a sensitive register of emotions, and clutching my long leather satchel in those smelly stores, I looked with surprise at the grown-up world into which I had crept, that part of it, at least, exposed to me undisguised in this strange, foreign quarter of Ottawa. The scene is as bright and as audible to me today as it was when I made my way that winter long ago through the snow and into those works and shops that were all so redolent of their trades.

One night in January I saw an advertisement in the *Ottawa Journal* for a clerk in the Imperial Munitions Board, offering a salary of $50 a month, double what I was getting. Next day, with my bank satchel under my arm, I went and applied for the vacancy. I was no more than half in earnest; the fabulous sum of $50 drove my steps there. The man who interviewed me did so only perfunctorily, and after an enquiry about my very brief working past, said 'O.K. I guess you'll do. When can you start?' When I told my father that night, he was very pleased. 'Fancy doubling your salary in that way, Rache! You'll get on in the world, old son. You are going to be a rich man one day.'

'What will Mr. Hamilton say, Dad?'

A cloud crossed my father's expressive face. 'That's my problem, son. He can't take it out on you.'

It was a tedious job after the romantic one of being a bank messenger. I sat all day at a desk entering up purchases on cards, and it seemed to me that the hours dragged and that five o'clock each day would never come. I walked home through the wintry streets, glad to stretch my long legs, to feel the frost on my face, to see the brilliantly-lit stores. Down Sparks Street, along Bank Street, then into the relative darkness of Maclaren Street. The lights would fade and with them my spirits, knowing that the flat would be empty and in darkness, and that ahead of me stretched an evening as purposeless as the day had been. Why did I have no friends? Why was I alone? If only I had someone to love, someone to whom I could pour out all the strange and powerful emotions that pushed like the surge of a flood through my mind, how happy I would be in this fairy land, so beautiful now in the first white months of winter.

When the longer spring evenings came it was harder for me, for the smell of earth and springtime came to shake my thin young frame into a frenzy. I experienced a restlessness that was like a sickness. I started thinking of running away to sea. I could make my way to Montreal, sign on a boat and leave this lonely city and my loveless home for ever. I was nearly on the point of doing this when a simpler plan occurred to me. On my walks I had noticed that the 74th Battery of the R.C.A. had its headquarters in a park on the outskirts of the city. One Saturday afternoon I went up to the Guard Room at the gate and said I wanted to enlist. I was taken through to the Orderly Room where an officer asked me my name and my age. I hesitated over the latter for a second or two and then said eighteen.

He looked at me sharply. 'These kids,' he said to the sergeant. 'Do you think you are the only hero in this country? You'll have to produce a birth certificate, you know, so you might as well tell the truth.'

'It's in Australia,' I said.

He smiled. 'Well, that's a new excuse. You'll have to have a letter from your father, then. Will he give it? Where is he and what does he do?'

I was anxious now only to leave and not get further involved in prevarication. I said, 'I'll see my father and ask him if he'll give me a letter and then I'll come back.'

He said, 'Yes, you do that, feller. And don't be in any hurry. This war is going to last a long time yet.'

I could not keep this adventure from my father. There was so little to talk to him about these days, and I thought that the encounter, though brief, showed me in a favourable light. The lie I had told about my age was for an heroic purpose. Of course he would not give the letter, nor did I want him to. I had signified my restlessness and unhappiness; it would be enough if he felt sorry for me. I did not know what I expected him to say, but imagining the scene as one does a moment before one precipitates it, I thought, 'That will make him think. I might have gone, and that might have been the end of me!'

But my father never did anything that anyone expected. He laughed. 'Good God,' he said, 'that was a spunky thing to do.'

'You can only die once,' I said. I had begun to use

large portentous phrases of this kind when talking to
my father, I suppose in order to win his approval.

'That's the way to look at life,' he said, and smiled
at me, picked up the *Journal*, swung his long legs onto
the stool. 'You're very like your Uncle Rache,' he
said. 'He went to sea on an impulse.' Then he read
his paper.

I sat with my hands tightly clasped between my
knees. I could feel throbbing inside me something that
had not been there ever before. I was terrified of death,
having seen it recently at close quarters. But something
almost physical was impelling me forward to the brink
where one leaves life and is flung upon the space that is
death. I had almost to exert muscular pressure to resist
it as I sat there. My father raised his paper, his gold
pince-nez perched on the thin bridge of his nose. The
aroma of his cigar was redolent of life, of the life that I
clung to, and longed for.

I got up and went into the bedroom which Clive
and I shared. He was reading in bed. I looked at
myself in the mirror, turning my head this way and
that, trying to see myself as others must see me. Was I
going mad, was I repellent to people, was I of no
interest to anyone except myself? Clive said, 'What
are you looking at?' 'Who do you think?' I replied.
'Me, of course.'

A month later, in March, I did run away, this time
in earnest, following plans which I had carefully made.
I had given in my notice at the office, telling the manager
that I was going to join the Air Force in Toronto. As
a matter of fact I meant only to join up if I found I
could not get a job, but it sounded somehow more
tactful to give out as immediate intention what was in

fact only to be an ultimate and desperate step. The results of this might have taught me a lesson if I had been capable of learning from them.

For the dozen people in that office, men and women thirty to sixty years old, incapable themselves because of age or ill-health of taking an active part in the War, were evidently stirred by the prospect of my going off to it in my shining youth. They gathered their forces and combined their contributions to arrange a party, and unknown to me, until the appalling moment arrived, they had all chipped in to buy me a farewell present — a gold wrist-watch with, *horrors !*, an inscription on the back.

It was Prohibition time, but somebody had produced a few bottles of whisky; it was springtime and the whisky combined with vernal impulses in all those bodies now emerging from the wrappings, the woolly scarves, the felt overshoes, the heavy coats in which they had been bundled all winter, to make a very merry party. There was high-pitched laughter, there was a little amorousness, there was an oration in my favour by the manager, there were clappings of hands and cheers; and there was I, standing holding this gold watch, my heart thudding, my hands wet with an agony of shyness; there was I being assailed with clamorous cries and shouted at to make a speech. I couldn't have made a speech if I had had one prepared. All I could do was wave my arms like tentacles and grin from ear to ear, and shake my head, until somebody handed me a little glass of raw whisky, and I took a swallow, and nearly died of the shock. I was led, shaking and coughing, from the room.

How slow one is to learn. I thought this was the

most touching tribute that had ever been paid by a band
of friends to one of their circle, but now age and dis-
illusionment tell me that I was probably merely the
excuse for a good party. Yet this little celebration
altered slightly the direction of my life. With a gold
watch and this splendid inscription, how could I go only
and look for a job in Toronto? My mind was made
up. I would join the R.A.F. as soon as I got to Toronto,
and try to be a hero and to live up to the fine conception
these wonderful people had of me.

The next morning, when I reached Toronto, I did
not go to look for a room as I had intended doing, but
went straight to the Armouries, and offered myself to
the Royal Air Force. It was the end of March in 1918,
and conscription had just come in in Canada. The recruiting offices of every service were being besieged by
young farm boys and woodsmen who had hung back
while enlistment was still voluntary, but who now
wanted to anticipate being drafted. Forty or fifty of
us raw youths were at the Armoury Gates on a cold
spring morning before they were opened. We were
swept in, made to fill forms, told then to strip, and
stood about naked as fledgelings waiting for the medical
examination. It was four o'clock that afternoon before
I put on my clothes again, and meanwhile I had passed
through some unutterably embarrassing moments. I
had never been medically examined before, and I burnt
with shame at some of the rough and familiar treatment
given to parts of my anatomy that it was not extraordinary to think of as very private. Probing fingers,
squeezing hands, searched me for weaknesses, and where
my body was not blue with cold it felt red with shame.
In one room a bearded sergeant handed me a glass flask.

I did not know what I was expected to do with it, whether to spit in it or go and fill it with water. It seemed better to ask than to do the wrong thing, so I said, 'Excuse me, sergeant, what am I to do with this ?'

'Pee in it, you silly bugger, what do you suppose ?' he growled at me, and the shock was so great it took a moment or two of concentration to unseal the tap inside me.

But I was passed, and with most of the others was marched away across the city to Jesse Ketchum's School, where we were installed in bunks and given a uniform, and were allowed to wander about disconsolately for a day. I seized the opportunity to telephone my father. I had left a note which he would have got on his return home last night, telling him that I was leaving for Toronto to join the R.A.F., and that I would telephone him as soon as I was settled, but I could not imagine him as greatly concerned. I felt reasonably sure that he would be relieved to have got me off his hands. It was not want of affection for any of us that made him like this, but a desperate desire to be free of us and to lead his own life.

My inner conviction was right. He said, 'Sure you're all right, old chap ? Good luck to you. They'll be giving you some leave some time. Let us know how you get along.'

I told him on the 'phone of the gold watch the office had given me. 'Splendid,' he said; 'they must have been very fond of you. I'm not surprised. By the way, what age did you tell them you were ?' I said eighteen years and eleven months, three years more than I actually was.

He laughed. 'You must almost be the youngest

man in the Army,' he said. 'God bless you, old son. Be a good boy.'

With which customary valediction our conversation ended, and I returned to my bunk, at peace with the world, satisfied now that I had left childhood behind me, and was a man.

CHAPTER SIX

S o, at the age of fifteen, I found myself a cadet-officer in the Royal Air Force, and my chief anxiety was that my age should not be discovered. In those first few days in Jesse Ketchum's School I took every precaution, whistling while I went through the unnecessary process of shaving so that nobody's suspicions should be aroused by the fact that the razor slid silently over my smooth cheeks. The talk in the barracks was considerably above my head, but I laughed at jokes I could not follow, and nobody seemed to notice that I did not contribute anything to the record which seemed to be almost exclusively concerned with sex. The authorities, swamped with the big intake of the last month, collected us together every day and gave us lectures, illustrated by lantern slides, on the effects of venereal disease. All this was new to me, and very frightening. When a man in the bunk next to me was taken off to hospital one night with a venereal complication, I was terrified that I might have caught it simply by sleeping next to him. For days I was dry-mouthed and apprehensive. I had not reckoned with this as one of the risks of war.

Then one day we were paraded and addressed by the Station Commander. He said that training was being cut down, and that those of us who had come in since the end of March would be sent on leave for three months. We could go back to our homes and our jobs, but we must be ready to return at the end of that time, or before then if summoned. We would be on the R.A.F. Reserve, unpaid, but subject to instant recall.

Everybody, I think, except me was delighted at this turn of events. I might have been, too, except for the presentation gold watch, the tribute to my anticipated heroism. How I wished that it had never been given to me. It was like the albatross in the Ancient Mariner's tale, a memento of a rash act which nothing could obliterate. I went to the Orderly Room, and said that for personal reasons I could not return home, and as I hadn't more than my few days' pay saved, could they help me to get a temporary job? They said, 'Sure, boy, if you want to work on a farm. Have you had any farming experience?'

I said I certainly had, that I had worked at the Dominion Experimental Farm in Ottawa. O.K., they said, how about Peterborough? Know that district? Here's a man called Earle wants help, offers $30 a month and keep. I said it would suit me fine. They gave me a railway warrant, and said they would notify him, and they wrote down that address as one to which my recall papers would be sent. With a sigh of relief at a danger avoided, I left the Orderly Room, and three days later I was on a train to Peterborough.

Nightfall on the quiet Ontario farm-lands. The scent of fresh earth invigorated me when I stepped down from the hot, odorous day-coach onto Peterborough platform. Outside the station was a farm-cart, and standing beside it an immense man, Tom Earle, who had come to meet me. I could not see him clearly in the glimmering dusk, but I liked his voice and felt his

friendliness as I sat beside him and we jogged our way
through the empty countryside under the glittering stars.

A warm welcome awaited me in the lamp-lit
kitchen. Tom Earle was revealed in the light of the
kitchen to be a handsome young giant of about twenty-
five or thirty, burnt brick-red by the sun. He introduced his wife, a pale slip of a woman with rimless
eye-glasses, an old farmer in overalls, his father, and a
white-haired, sweet-faced woman, his mother. They
fussed over me, and made me feel at home, and said I
must be starving. Tom's wife, who was called Edith,
flew to the stove. Tom took me up to my room, and
poured water into a basin from a ewer for me to wash,
and then left me, telling me to come down to supper as
soon as I could. I looked about me with an enormous
feeling of contentment. The room was so clean it was
shining, and smelt of beeswax and furniture polish.
There was a crocheted carpet on the floor and a knitted
quilt across the narrow bed. The linen was blinding
white, and shiny with starch. The window was open
to the night, and when I leaned out of it I could smell
the sweet scent of the stable yard, and hear the grunting
of the farm beasts in the still darkness.

Supper was a huge plate of mashed potatoes, covered
with fried eggs, and cups of green tea. It tasted good,
except for the tea, which was like medicine. Old Mrs.
Earle was overjoyed at my appetite. She said I was
much too thin, and needed building up. They asked
me questions about my family, and when I said that my
mother was dead, Mrs. Earle said, 'Poor boy, you look
lonely and neglected. We will try to make this a home
for you.' And I felt so moved by this expression of
kindness, the first that I had heard for a long time, that

I could have cried if I hadn't felt so sleepy and well-fed, like a cat that has had its milk and wants to curl up and forget the world.

It seemed to me that I had only been asleep for an hour before Tom Earle was pulling at my leg, and telling me it was time to get up. It was five o'clock and still dark. I stumbled downstairs and joined him in the yard where we sluiced ourselves at a trough fitted with a hand-pump. Then he showed me the field where the cows were and we drove them into the barn, and for an hour we sat with our foreheads dug into the warm flanks, our hands working ceaselessly at the teats. My wrists, unaccustomed to this exercise, ached with pain, but whenever I stopped for a moment Tom Earle's big head would come up, and I realized from a smouldering look in his eyes that he wasn't at all times the benevolent giant I had taken him for the night before, and I bent to my task again.

The days succeeded one another, and I saw nobody else except these four people save on Sundays when we all drove in the buggy to church a few miles away. It surprised me that we then talked to nobody, but sat by ourselves, and merely exchanged a distant nod of greeting with neighbours when we came out of church and were backing the horse into the shafts and adjusting the traces before setting off along the dusty road to the farm again. Once or twice the minister came back to Sunday dinner with us, but he was no company, being a sad dyspeptic man with odious table manners and a sepulchral voice which gave me the shivers, and which he used only to retail gossip and scandal about what went on in neighbouring parishes under his unhealthy observation, but not under his care.

As the summer heat grew in intensity, and the days lengthened, we cut the hay, and were out in the fields from early morning until the last light had gone. Then we had to water the horses and bed them down, before stumbling in to sit sagging wearily over the kitchen table and eat our supper. Mrs. Earle said that I was working too hard for my age, and that Tom ought to let up on me a little, but Tom, who had so impressed me at our first meeting with a sense of kindness, but who appeared now always irritable and jumpy, said I was being paid a man's wage and must expect to do a man's work. Edith, with a sidelong glance at her husband, declared that her mother-in-law was spoiling me, and a little smouldering hostility now and then flared up at the table and made us all shift uneasily on the hard benches on which we sat. I began to notice that whenever there was an errand on which somebody had to be sent, Edith commanded me to do it, to fetch a few logs for the oven, or to get another pail of water from the well. Mrs. Earle, bursting with motherliness, would try to do it for me, but Edith stood between us and commanded me to go. She fascinated me, this thin pale woman in her print dress, with black hair wound tightly against the nape of her white neck, her eyes restless and hostile behind her glasses. Upstairs in bed at night, I would hear her and Tom moving about in their room. They had been married only a little while; they must, in their huge double bed which I could see through the open door when I passed it during the day, have made love and have had moments when they were lost to the whole world. But they must quickly have hurried back to the demands of everyday life. I never saw them soft with each other, or exchanging an amor-

ous glance, or touch each other with playful, uncon-
trollable gestures such as escape young lovers sometimes
in company. He was generally bad-tempered in the
morning, and he had only me to take it out on.

At my mechanical and heavy tasks in the field all
day, fired and burnt in the furnace of the sun, my
sweat-soaked body dragged itself wearily after the hay-
wagon, and the only thing that distinguished me from
the animals pulling it was that I had a mind. It worked
steadily, and often followed channels which I had occasionally had glimpses of before, as though of a mirage
shimmering in the desert, and from which I had turned
back with a thudding heart and a sense of shame. The
long hours spent under the hot sun, the intimate close-
ness of our lives to the animals we worked and tended,
the lack of anyone of my own age to talk these matters
over with, made my imagination follow vistas which
my body was too tired and lax now to forbid. It was
in such a state, at the end of haying time, that I cele-
brated my sixteenth birthday. I did not say anything
to the Earles about it. They knew my Army age, and
in some odd way it seemed to me as though I would
add to the dimensions of my prevarication to put now
another year to the tally. So I kept quiet. It was the
first birthday in my life which had been unacknowledged
and unrecognized; I don't think I heard even from my
father.

I wonder now what the Earles thought of me, a
lanky youth with eyes as large as a young calf's, speaking
in an accent quite different from theirs, not skilled in
farm work, and too often when talkative, boasting of
the glories and comforts of the home remembered in
the past, of a mother's love, and a father's good looks

and reputation. I think that Mr. and Mrs. Earle saw through this, and tolerated my air of superiority, but Edith resented it, and worked Tom up to resenting it, and on a hot night at the end of July when bone-weary we sat at supper, with two hours' work still before us in the distant field we were cutting, the climax came. The smouldering hostility burst suddenly into flame. Edith, her pallor accentuated by the heat, the dark rings under her eyes discernible behind the rimless glasses she wore, had been specially hostile to me that evening. It is very probable that I had been specially tiresome. Anyhow, we contradicted each other at every opportunity, and had even each begun to make assertive, aggressive remarks to each other, remarks which invited contradiction, just to get one another's goat, as the Canadian expression so vividly puts it. Suddenly Edith made an assertion which passed the limits of my small stock of patience.

'What bloody nonsense you talk,' I said, anger at her rising in me irresistibly.

There was an appalled moment of silence. I saw their faces, open-mouthed at what I had said, swim before my angry gaze. This was 1918, and 'bloody', everywhere in the English-speaking world, but especially in Ontario, was not a word to use in the presence of ladies, and I knew it. But my temper was throbbing like a pulse in my head, and I looked down at my plate and waited for the storm to break. In the midst of my confusion and shame, I could not resist an awful joy that I had shocked into speechlessness the pale vapid face of this woman whom I knew now that I hated, and hated with all the passion of a nerve-racked, bodily exhausted, adolescent boy.

The storm broke immediately. Edith drew back her chair from the table; her mouth stretched wide, showing her teeth. 'Did you hear him, Tom? Did you hear what he said? Hit him, beat him, give him a hiding, Tom. Beat him into pulp, the dirty creature. If you don't, I will.'

She clawed at Tom's shoulder, her glasses fell forward on her nose and she had to free a hand to set them right again. I looked open-mouthed at her. Tom's face turned a dusky red, and he glared at me, and I saw his great hand curl into a menacing fist. I was frightened, not of that, but of the storm I had raised, and yet I could not say that I was sorry, though I longed to say to Mrs. Earle, whose eyes were moist with tears, that I was sorry to have disappointed her. The spell was broken when Tom pushed aside his wife and said gruffly to me, 'Come outside.'

I followed him out of the kitchen door. Then he grabbed me by the shoulder and said, 'You filthy young beast, using language like that. Before you go back and apologize to my wife and my parents, I'm going to teach you a lesson. Take that, you dirty young bastard,' and he hit me with the flat of his hand across my mouth.

For a brief moment the smarting pain was uppermost in my thoughts, then the appalling indignity of what was being done to me made me gibber with rage. He was a head taller and a good many pounds heavier than I was, but I flung myself at him, hitting him wherever I could. These puny blows he brushed aside with a huge derisive arm, caught my neck in the crook of his other arm and bending me against his leg, flung me to the ground. Then he squatted on top of me,

I

pinning my arms beneath his knees. As I cried out at this fresh indignity, I heard the kitchen door open and saw Edith bending over his shoulder and looking down at me.

'Hit him, hit him, the dirty beast,' she cried.

I strained against Tom, and yelled. Then he hit me three or four times in the face until I ceased to struggle. He got up and I lay there crying, and they went in, shutting the kitchen door after them, and there was no sound from behind the door, but only in the yard the sound of my racking sobs, to which after a moment I found myself listening as though the noise came from someone else, and I was standing there looking on. I got up slowly and painfully, and walked away to the fields. Night was beginning to fall. I knew that I was never going back to that house. I was alone and friendless and without cover in a darkening world.

CHAPTER SEVEN

I SLEPT the night in the fields, not on Tom Earle's property but on a farm near the town. Then in the white misty dawn I got up, feeling stiff and bruised and hungry. I had seven dollars in my pocket. I had six weeks' wages coming to me, but I did not mean to go back and collect them, and I hoped the seven dollars would be enough to get me to Toronto. I was still in my overalls, but I had a good wash in the station, and I felt more hopeful, and also more angry, as I waited on the platform for the early train to come in. Sitting there in the sunlight of the fresh summer morning, I thought over my life, the way that I had come, and the way that I was going, and I made up my mind never to go hungry or be helpless or dependent on others again. Life was hard; well, I would be hard too. Life was unkind; then I need not waste time feeling sentimental about people. My father evidently did not care what happened to me; well, I wouldn't go home until I could go as a successful man, with a fortune made or with medals won in this war. I felt bitter at the treatment I had received, and I longed for some vindictive action. I meant to make Tom Earle sorry for what he had done. As I sat there, I was framing in my thoughts the letter I was going to send him. As always, I fell back on words, the sound and power of them, my ever-loving companions in time of trouble.

They did not fail me in this, the first instance in which I put them to use.

When I got to Toronto I bought a pen, a writing-pad and some envelopes, and then went to a small hotel. Up in my room I sat down at the dressing-table and pulled the paper towards me. An hour later I was satisfied with the letter I had written. I asked for my clothes to be sent on, my back wages amounting to $45 to be sent to me by return of post, and then added that I was consulting a solicitor about the damages I could claim for assault. If Earle had any suggestions to make, he should let me know about this right away before we took action.

For two days I had nothing to eat except coffee and toast, and most of the time, in order to keep my appetite unstimulated, I lay on my bed reading a second-hand copy of *Pickwick Papers* I had bought for 25 cents. On the third morning there was a letter from Tom Earle, and enclosed with it a cheque for $75. He said he was sorry for what had happened, that they had been very worried when I had not returned home that night, and that next morning they had even notified the police of my disappearance. He was glad to know I was all right, and he was sending a cheque for an additional month's wages in lieu of notice. My clothes were being sent to me in a separate parcel.

For the moment I felt triumphant, but I soon realized that seventy-five dollars would not last me long. I would have to look for another job, but before I did that I thought I would see if the R.A.F. would allow me to resume my cadet's training. After my experience with the Earles, I did not want to go into another farmer's home.

I reported to the Armouries that morning. After I had waited round for a few hours they found my file. I was interviewed by an officer. He was a friendly and understanding man, and I told him without, I think, undue exaggeration what my experience had been with the Earles, and how much I wanted to renew my training. He sent me before a board of officers who asked me questions about my past, and at twelve o'clock I was told that I could resume training, and was given a pass to get me to Long Branch Camp.

Once again I was issued with a uniform, and at the age of sixteen found myself again actively serving my King and country. The transformation from the lonely life on the farm, with the unhappy atmosphere of the last month, to the noisy din of a barrack room was extremely comforting. I made friends, and spent some exciting evenings out in Toronto, proud of my uniform and my manhood, hoping only that I would not have to get involved, and thereby show my complete inexperience, in any of the adventures with women about which my friends were continually talking.

There was one amongst this group of men who flattered me by paying particular attention to me. His name was Steve MacDonough, and he came from Winnipeg. He was about twenty, rather small, with dark hair, a brown complexion, blue eyes and very attractive, even teeth, which showed only when he smiled. This he did rarely, being quiet and self-contained. But he was liked by all the men, and when we did come into contact with women at the King Edward Hotel in Toronto, I noticed that they all paid particular attention to him, though he appeared less interested in them than any of our party. He spoke as infrequently as he smiled. He seemed content just to tag along with us, watching us with his deep-blue eyes, drinking with us, gazing in a distant fashion at the harpies who attached themselves to us in the hotel, responding with an occasional slow smile which transformed his whole face to their attempts to flirt with him, and watching me, I noticed with some embarrassment and at the same time with a feeling of pleasure, whenever I broke the bounds of my shyness and made an attempt to join in the party spirit.

As the weeks passed in camp, we began to talk to one another. He asked me about my life, and I told him what I had to tell. He told me of his own life in Winnipeg, where he lived with his father, who was a widower, as mine was. We discovered no mutual interests; he never read a book, I was always reading them, even in the spare hours when I could lie on my bunk. He would lie beside me, doing absolutely nothing, smoking cigarette after cigarette, staring into space. When I put down my book he would start to talk. When I took it up again he would light another cigarette. Sometimes I would steal a glance at him, but his face would be completely expressionless. He appeared to be thinking of nothing, not even daydreaming. It amazed me that anybody could be like that, but it was pleasant to have him near me. He was the first friend I had made in Canada, and I could feel a fondness for him, strange as he was, growing on me with each hour we spent in this uncommunicative way.

In the middle of September it was apparent that the war would soon be over, and rumours were rife in the camp that we were to be discharged and sent home. Mac and I discussed the prospect. He told me that he did not mean to go back to Winnipeg, that he was going to stay in the East and find a job. I told him that I did not mean to go home either, and we decided that as soon as we were let out we would go to Montreal, where Mac had heard that there was good money to be made at Vickers' shipyards.

A week went by, and the rumours thickened, and were passed among us by people with some claim to be in the know, clerks from the Orderly Room, and a sergeant in charge of our hut. Then one morning we were paraded and addressed by the commanding officer. He said that there now seemed no prospect of our getting our commissions, that those of us who wanted to return to civil life could apply for discharge and that the remainder would be transferred to other units. By this time nearly all of us were ready to go. Mac and I applied for discharge, and a few days later found ourselves in civilian clothes in Toronto, ready to come to grips with the world.

And there was the end of my short career as an airman. I came out of the Royal Air Force with a discharge certificate on which was written 'Not Finally Approved'. The words were a testament of failure. I was terribly ashamed of it, and any time during the next year or two when I had to produce it to get a job I felt the rush of the shame. But no one else seemed to notice it. They did not know that I had got no nearer learning to fly than some weeks of tedium at Jesse Ketchum's School and at Long Branch Camp. The Germans were on the run — it was now October 1918 — and it was plain that it was not worth while joining anything else.

It was a six- or seven-hour journey by train to

Montreal. We had travel warrants, our saved-up pay and a small gratuity each. To me it was more money than I had ever had in my life, and I would have been extravagant with it and gone to a good hotel in Montreal while I investigated the job. But Mac was of a much more cautious disposition. That meant no lunch on the train, to which I had been looking forward; we satisfied our hunger with purchases from the 'peanut butcher' as he is called, the functionary in a red cap who patrols ceaselessly up and down the day coaches of Canadian trains, with a basket of his wares slung in front of him, crying 'R-rinjes, char-klit, peanuts'.

When we reached Windsor station in Montreal it was mid-afternoon. The day was beautiful, the air clean and cold and delicious to breathe after the odorous heat of the day coach. We came out onto the square in front of the station, and I looked for the first time at the mountain rising up from the city, appearing to be only a block or two away, brilliant with the red and gold of autumn, clear-cut against the deep blue of the sky. I was in French Canada; it was like being in Paris. All around me a new world moved, vivid in colour and promising excitement. But Mac said, 'Come on, feller.' He had it all figured out what street-car we should take to Maisonneuve, the eastern suburb where Vickers' shipyards lay. The ride was long and tedious; it passed for miles through the French part of Montreal, to the east of St. Lawrence Boulevard. The houses were different from most of those I knew in Ottawa and Toronto. They were excessively ugly, but they were practical. Usually they were duplex houses, the upper part having a broad iron staircase which ran down at a wide angle to the ground in front of the lower part.

The people in the streets looked very French; the street-car notices and advertisements were all in French, and the conductor's English was not as good as my school French. I had the advantage here of Mac, who hadn't a word of French and who was contemptuous of all pea-soupers, as he called them. He pointed out to me with a nudge and a sardonic grin the priests who were certainly very plentiful in the streets, saying 'Quebec Highlanders'.

At the entrance to the shipyards there were iron gates, guarded by a policeman. Mac and I said we were looking for work. We were shown the door to the works office, and entered an outer waiting-room. A little window shot up and a man with a green eye-shade asked us what we wanted. We said work, and he asked for our discharge certificates, looked at them — cursorily, I was glad to note. He told us that he could take us on as drillers' helpers at 27½ cents an hour and that we could start at seven in the morning with No. 8 gang. Having done all this and taken down our names while he held the wooden window open with one elbow, he let it drop; and within two minutes of our entering the door of the office we were in the street again, fully accredited employees of Vickers' shipyards.

'Time-and-a-half overtime, double time after midnight,' Mac said, as we made our way to a restaurant opposite the gates. 'We should be able to pull down fifty to sixty bucks a week.'

I couldn't figure this rapidly, but I was perfectly prepared to take Mac's word for it.

The restaurant he led me into, opposite the works, was a Chinese one. We ordered pork chops and fried potatoes and coffee. When the Chinaman brought it,

Mac, who had been looking at 'rooms to let' in the *Star*, said :

'Say, Charley, we just got ourselves jobs at the ship-yards, starting tomorrow. Know where we can get a room round here ? You got a food card for customers eating regular at your joint ?'

Sure, the Chinaman knew all the tricks. In his sing-song voice, his Chinese lisp blent with a Canadian accent, he issued us each with a food card which had twenty-one little squares round its edges, one of which would be punched after each meal. At 22 Marie-Thérèse Street we might find a room :

'Mrs. Boucher, sure, she takee lot of workers, heaps plenty, sure.'

What I hadn't bargained for was a double bed in a small, poky room. But it was no worse than the cramped quarters of barracks, and the rent asked by Mrs. Boucher was certainly very cheap. $3.50 a week for the room, to be divided half and half with Mac, and 25 cents each for twenty-one meals on the food card ; this meant that I could eat three meals a day and have a bed to sleep in, all for $4.25 a week. And if, as Mac prophesied, I could earn $50 or $60 a week, it wouldn't take me long to set aside a very nice little sum.

Led on by Mac, I found myself settling into an un-comfortable but profitable life. At six each morning the works hooter would blow a siren blast, and all around us, up and down the street, as well as on every floor of Mrs. Boucher's house, the living creatures would stir from sleep and groan their way into con-ciousness As November crept in and the days shortened, I would hear up and down the street the bang of windows being closed against the cold air of the morning ; and then the gathering cough. It began with the clearing of innumerable throats, like an orchestra tuning up for a performance ; then the cough erupting like percussion instruments, singular and solitary at the start, then gathering strength as a chorus does, till all up and down the street there would be a barrage of shaken frames rattling and echoing in the early morning darkness, until one caught the sound of some lingering painful paroxysm, so ultimate, so stretched to the limit of endurance, that one's eyes watered in sympathy and one's own thin chest felt constricted with torture.

We came out into the air to get our breakfast. It was often misty at this time of the year ; it was cold and repellent always. Then in the grey light of the morning we would make our way to Charley's. Here yellow, naked light poured from the unshaded bulbs, and dark-visaged workers, wearing their capes and hats, ate with rapacity and gulped their cups of coffee. The smell of ham and fried eggs, of cigarettes and incompletely washed bodies, of grease-stained mackinaws sweating in the heat, of coffee and buttered toast, mingled and wreathed its way throughout the atmosphere of the room.

I was always ready for my breakfast, being young and healthy, and not yet having become a serious smoker. Sometimes the close atmosphere of Charley's would threaten to overcome me, but the moment of nausea passed quickly, and I grabbed for the food given to me. There was no choice. On a card, well — you took what they gave you. It was substantial, but badly cooked, and it stank of grease. But it was warming, and as the winter reached down from the north and grabbed the river the way you grab a snake, Charley's breakfasts became a symbol of warmth.

As the month advanced, the cold crowded in like a bully. Where it touched, the threat of what was to come was more painful than what one actually felt. But it was ominous and cruel.

My job was very simple, and so was Mac's. Our drillers worked their drills with compressed air. My job was to carry the air-hose from here to there on the ship on which we were working, and to carry in a leather bag the rivets which my mate would use to drive into the steel plates on which we worked.

Up and down the river there were five or six ships in various stages of completion, some mere timber shells of the shapes they were to become, others steel-plated, splashed with red lead, all ready for launching.

Winter was closing in fast. An open channel remained in the middle of the river, black and ugly in comparison with the white snow on either side of it, and here the swift water rushed its way to freedom and the open gulf a thousand miles below Montreal. Other channels, like dark vertebrae attached to this thick black spine, stretched towards the shore, and the remaining traffic on the river, small tugs and other little ships, puffed up and down these narrow highways. Close to the shore and to our shipyards the water was still open, and frantic efforts were being made to launch two vessels, almost ready to be released from the stocks, in order that new keels might be laid in these and work carried on with the nearly-completed hulls as they lay frozen by the shore during the winter. Rich was the overtime harvest for us all as the days grew shorter and colder and the ice put its stranglehold on the wide river.

Every day the wind blew steadily from the north,

every night the frost pushed the mercury down in the thermometer. Now, when Mac and I came out in the morning, often having worked till midnight the night before, the skies would be grey and a biting little wind would lift the shirt from my chest. It did not chill me, but it frightened me, remembering the winter before.

We would hurry round the corner to see the cheerful light streaming from Charley's, and the smell of Charley's coffee and frying bacon would lift spirits that had been briefly submerged by contact with the grey morning. It was lovely, that fifteen minutes' battle in the blinding light and homely smell of that cheap café before the five minutes to seven whistle would bring us streaming out into the cold again, crowding through the gates to our painful assignation with the day.

I did not much like my driller, Hart Brown. He was a Canadian from Ontario. It was a convention that every driller had had a dirty trick played on him when the Time Office had sent him his particular helper. Of all the stupid, lazy, forgetful bastards in the world, each driller's helper was the prize one. It was a form of fun which the bullies amongst them had established, and which gave each one a chance to kick his particular helper around publicly, so to speak, and with the support of the others. Hart Brown was a bully, or so I thought. Mac was luckier with Pierre Bisson, a French-Canadian from Quebec, a large white man with a black moustache, whose thoughts were always on women, and whose speech was exclusively concerned with them, so that he had little left with which to abuse Mac.

I could see that my accent was going to get me into trouble with Hart Brown and if he didn't like my large and apprehensive blue eyes and my unshaven red cheeks,

I didn't at all like his cold grey eyes, always slightly bloodshot, or the way his lips were always moving. Like many of the workers in the shipyards, he chewed tobacco continuously. Perhaps this had kept his lips in perpetual motion, but it looked to me, too, when I sometimes found his baleful eye fixed on me and I saw those lips silently writhing, that they were uttering threats of what he meant to do to me when he got me into some dark corner of the hold; and the effect on my skin was exactly the same as that left by the early morning wind when it lifted my shirt — not cold exactly, but an apprehension of trouble to come.

We would collect our drills and hoses and meet our drillers at the jobs assigned to them for the day. There was something here in the luck of the draw. On a day when the wind had bared its fangs and was crouched with its ears flat back snarling at us from the north, it was a blessing to be given a job below decks, out of the wind's way, where we worked under electric bulbs enclosed in cages and swung on long cords. This was work likely to lead to trouble between the driller and his helper because, except when the light could be hung by its cage on some convenient hook, the helper had to hold it, and woe betide the poor bastard if he didn't hold it just exactly right. But sometimes, when the wind blew outside, it was worth it for the sake of shelter to lie up alongside Hart Brown on some confined slope below deck, holding the light on an arm that ached as much from anxiety as from the muscular effort, just to be out of the way of the wind, and to bury one's thoughts beneath the shattering din of rivets being driven into the steel plates in a confined quarter: such days that were steel-grey and angry with the moan of the wind were often followed by days on which winter came on, marching majestically, with all the trappings and the glory which stories read in childhood had taught me to expect. Beautiful are those Canadian days, with the sky a flawless blue of great beauty and depth, an inverted bowl of the purest colour imaginable, placed over the world. The sun had little warmth left in it; it was a round patch, pale orange in colour, on the blue of the sky. Before us the majestic river locked now in ice; behind us the Laurentian Mountains, shoulders to the sky; and ahead of us, on the other side of the river, the green forests stretching away to the south and east. You could see on the heights the clean white snow that lies in undisturbed and lonely places, glittering bright with a thousand pricks of light. In imagination you could smell the balsam branches bruised by its fall, though the nearest woods were miles from where our skeleton ships lay in their wooden frames. Under our feet, as the day went on, the ship's plates would become freezing cold, especially if we worked after 5 P.M., spurred on by the prize of time-and-a-half to midnight. My fingers holding the hose would ache with the sheer agony of cold; and my thin frame would feel as if the cold bellies of snakes were shifting on it. But the light was worth it, the exquisite light. For when the blue of this serene sky faded into blackness and I could no longer make out the green in the forests beyond the river, the wine-coloured shades of an early winter's evening would fall on this old town and its great river, and cold though I was, I could bear it.

★

The two hulls were ready for launching only just in time. In the last week of November a notice was put up on the Time Office board that Jobs Nos. 368 and 370 would be launched on Thursday afternoon at two-thirty by a lady with a name in the presence of a distinguished company, and the management would like to congratulate us on the fine effort we had made to complete these jobs in time. The language of the announcement was unexceptionable, and when I read it I felt quite a thrill of pride. But the notice might have been a calculated insult from the way in which our particular little gang of drillers received it. We goddamned this, we goddamned that, we spat profanity, we festooned the management with frightful parodies of their proclamatory style, so that I was in despair at the thought that I would not see my first launching, and of the hull which I had come to know so well.

I don't know about the hull, but I certainly did not know my drillers as I thought I did. Their response to the notice had been the automatic reaction of the worker at that time to boss language. They were not going to miss a free show, especially when they were being paid time for it.

The whistles screamed at one o'clock their summons back to work, and work on we did until two o'clock. Then three short blasts on the main siren advised us that we could lay down tools until after the ceremony. During the lunch hour I had walked up onto the foredeck of the ship lying next to the two about to be launched, and had picked myself out a vantage point from which to view the ceremony. I could do nothing about staking it, but when the hooter blew I rushed away, and pushing myself through the crowd, came

out on the foredeck with the first men to get there. I
sat with my legs hanging over the side, not fifty feet
from the launching platform, watching enviously the
little wickerwork chairs painted in gold, the profusion
of flowers, the gaily-coloured silk ribbons which arched
from the prow of the ship to the table, which were
destined to hold the bottle of champagne. It was very
cheerful, very delicate, very vivid, a little splash of gay
colour in a desert of rusty iron lit by coke fires.

The distinguished party came onto the platform. I
have forgotten who they were; I have forgotten them
all except one, a girl of my own age, the daughter
probably of someone very important, perhaps of the
middle-aged lady with the tight mouth and painted lips
who took up the bottle and, with the nonchalance of
an old hand, let it swing smack against the steel sides,
starting Job No. 368 on its long slide down into the
cold embrace of water.

She, this girl, the object of my absorbed attention,
wore a fur coat and had brown hair cut in the close
crop that was fashionable in 1919. Short skirts, too,
were fashionable, and her legs fascinated me.

The girl was bored; she was very pretty and she
was plainly bored. There was no one of her age in this
party; she had obviously been brought along against
her will, and an attractive sulkiness was manifest on her
little heart-shaped face as she sat slumped in her chair,
her hands stuck deep in the pockets of her fur coat, her
legs shining in the light and one folded over the other,
kicking impatiently at the air during the speeches.

I had never seen anything like her in my short life;
she was beauty itself to me. She was as young as I was,
but she communicated something sophisticated to me:

K

she was the first woman I had seen as a woman and as nothing else.

I could not take my eyes from her. Hardly breathing, I watched her with a completely absorbed attention, and so concentrated was my gaze that it had an effect I had not expected. She looked up at me, suddenly and directly, slightly frowning, for I could see the pucker of skin between her eyes, and I felt a sudden painful stab of shyness as she looked directly at me. Then her eyes fell away and I saw her shift in her chair. But once again, before she looked away finally, her eyes swung up to mine for a moment and I held myself frozen as one does when out with a gun and the game hears the crackling of a stick underfoot.

That contact had an effect upon my life. Suddenly it seemed to me frightful that I should be dressed like this, in greasy overalls and bathing but once a week, working as a clod merely for money's sake. Suddenly I wanted desperately to recross the gulf between my present circumstances and those of my upbringing. I wanted to get back to the point where I could talk to a girl like that, not sit as a greasy mechanic watching her across a void that was not fifty feet, but infinite in extent.

I read the advertisements in the Montreal *Star* each night, and one night found one which seemed to be just what I was looking for. 'Wanted,' it said, 'an Administrative Clerk in the Board of Pension Commissioners. Must be bilingual. Salary $1000 a year. Apply in writing to Mr. S. H. Elliott, Room 603, Windsor Building.'

I didn't know what an Administrative Clerk was, and I was uncertain of my right to describe myself as bilingual, but I certainly liked the sound of that one thousand dollars a year. I was making about $50 a week at the shipyards, but that meant working two or three nights a week till midnight; and occasionally, when the driller wanted more money, working through without a break from seven one morning until five the following evening. When I worked it out on paper I saw that a thousand dollars a year was only $20 a week, but on the other hand the hours would be easier and the work cleaner.

In response to my letter of application I was invited to call. I took a day off from the shipyards and spent the morning cleaning myself up, scrubbing my nails until they shone and having a hair-cut for a finishing touch. Fresh and pomaded, and by this time very keen to get the job, I presented myself for the interview. While I waited to go into Mr. Elliott's private office I looked at what I hoped were going to be my fellow-workers. They all looked so nice and clean; there was not a tough nor a mean face amongst them, and the office was beautifully warm. No doubt there were scores of people after this job, but I felt by this time I would do anything to get it. I was becoming fairly nervous by the time I was shown in to Mr. Elliott's room, but this was to stand me in good stead, as it turned out.

Mr. Elliott was then middle-aged, and I was sixteen, so I suppose that he has now long been gathered to his fathers and I can speak of him without restraint.

He had a tubby little figure, and he wore rimless eye-glasses, pince-nez fashion. He had grey hair parted

in the centre and he was going bald in front so that
when he threw his head back in an imperious gesture
— which was a little mannerism of his — you could
hardly see any hair at all, only his large grey eyes behind
the glasses looking down at you and compelling your
attention. He was a civil servant; he was pompous
and petty and cautious by instinct and training. He
had a large head and small pale hands and very little
feet for a man. He walked in rather an effeminate,
mincing manner. He had a way of laughing throatily,
yet when I got to know him better later, I found that
he had times of intense melancholy. He had no children,
but he was very paternalistic, and he treated his little staff
of about thirty as though they were his children.

When he heard my English accent I think he concluded that I had something to hide and had been sent
to Canada to hide it. But when I said my father had
been sent out to the Royal Mint, that we were Canadians by origin and were glad to be back, his attitude
changed.

'You don't know what a country we've got here,
boy. The surface barely scratched. You're nineteen.
By God, by the time you're my age there'll be twenty
million people living in Canada instead of seven
million. Now the war's over they'll come in their
thousands from every country in Europe, just pouring
in.

'Now let's see. Know what kind of a job this is?
It isn't all clerical, you know. Calls for something
more, calls for common sense and judgment. Let me
explain it. The widow of every Canadian soldier killed
on active service gets $40 a month for life, plus $12 for
the first child and $8 for every subsequent child. The

money comes to them in a cheque each month from Ottawa. Fine, as long as they behave themselves. But say they neglect the children, or drink, or go out on the streets ? Then Ottawa makes the pension payable through us, right here in this department. We have to manage their lives for them till they straighten up. Sometimes it's just temporary ; sometimes it looks as though it will be for ever. We have to see that they spend the money properly, feed and clothe the kids and send them to school. They're like patients, you see, kind of sick, morally sick; and we're like doctors trying to bring back regularity into lives that have become upset. Get it ?

'Well, your job will be to work on certain of these cases, trying to bring them back to a state of health, moral health. You'll work under Miss Bamford, you'll be one of her assistants. That is, if you're the successful applicant. I'll get her in anyway. She'd better have a look at you.'

Miss Bamford was a thin woman of fifty, flat-chested, with a warm-coloured skin, and laughing grey eyes behind a pair of glasses. When she spoke, she had a friendly voice and I thought, it will be nice working with her. It was to prove so, though at times she was as sharp with me as a mother with an erring child.

Back in Maisonneuve I waited three or four days, all the time longing for Mr. Elliott's letter, certain that these were my last days of agony on the frozen river, but cautious of giving up my job until I had the letter of appointment. I found the letter waiting for me on a Monday evening when I came back from work. There was no need to give notice, though I had told Mr.

Elliott that I would have to work out the balance of a week. But because of the vision I had had of St. Catherine Street I could not bear the thought of another six days of cold and tiredness, of Charley's greasy food, even of contact with Mac, who prophesied that on a thousand dollars a year I could never afford the laundry and tailor bills necessary to hold an office job. It was January, and the depth of winter. I was seized by a positive anguish to be clean and warm again, and I could not leave Maisonneuve quickly enough. I moved into the centre of Montreal and took a room at the Y.M.C.A.

Then began for me nine months of perfect happiness. A shaft of sunshine seemed to burst from the heavy clouds which had overhung my life since my mother's death. I cannot tell from whence the happiness came. I think it came partly from having a room to myself, and from eating clean food in the cafeteria of the Y.M.C.A. It came from the few friends I made in the Y, two or three who were a few years older than I was, knew far more of the world than I did, who protected me from evil without my really knowing it. Once or twice my own hunger for life might have carried me into swifter currents than I could have managed, but I was held back in a friendly, brotherly way by these men who did not prohibit for themselves the things which they forbade me.

Meanwhile, in the first few days at the office, Miss Bamford took me with her on her calls, showing me how to deal with these cases; then finally introduced me to my victims, explaining to them that I was to look after their affairs.

There were about ten names on my list, and the

addresses of all of them were in the poorer parts east of
St. Lawrence Boulevard, or in the French-Canadian
suburbs south of the St. Lawrence. I was not given
difficult cases to begin with — the number increased
greatly as the months passed by — and nearly all of
them were French, who in Miss Bamford's presence
stared at me as Red Indians must have stared at the
first white man in North America. I thought the
dumbfounded looks of incredulity with which they
acknowledged the introduction betokened disbelief that
anyone so youthful and inconsequential-looking (compared with Miss Bamford) could possibly deal with the
intricacy of their affairs. I tried to look very stern and
responsible as Miss Bamford went through their recent
affairs. But indeed they were sinners in a very small
way, and even at sixteen one could not possibly look
censorious at their little recitations of sin.

There was Mrs. Cartier who was just plain extravagant, and spent all her pension in a week if it came
directly to her; each week she had to confess her little
extravagances before another week's income was doled
out.

There was Mme Boileau, whose case was more
serious, but who was so very pretty and intelligent-
looking that it seemed each transgression must have
been an accident, who could not take a drink without
drinking a bottle, and who had twice got into trouble
on such occasions. Her pension was administered for
her because she would, as a sign of remorse, neglect the
child of her sin and the Administrative Clerk had to act
as foster-father.

There was Mme Daubeny, who had two quite
alarmingly pretty twin daughters of sixteen who were

to become both the bane and the intoxicant of my life. Mme Daubeny was odd; the Pensions Department doctor who examined her with her own doctor had told Miss Bamford that eventually she would have to go into a mental hospital. Meanwhile, rather than let the daughters spend the money on themselves, the pension was to be administered for her.

The rest were much the same, suffering from little failings and weaknesses which made them wards of the Pensions Department, and here was I set up to manage their affairs. Miss Bamford explained it carefully to me. They were to respect me; without their respect and their trust, in the end without their affection, I would be able to do nothing. They were to be made to behave, not to persist in their various transgressions, out of fear of my reproof, out of liking for me and anxiety to win my approval. I would be for them the 'government', the source from which their money came, the power that could withhold it. It was a relationship that called for the most delicate balance and management. They were bound to test my capacity for sternness, and I might look for some trials and disappointments at first, but she believed that I would get along very well with them and grow very fond of them in the end.

When I recall that year in Montreal I wonder that my father should have let me out upon the world at such an age without any advice as to how to cope with it, and without appearing to care whether or not I survived. And yet I know that he did care. His letters were always full of affection. But either he was totally unaware of the risks I was running, or thought it was best for me to run them and get them over with.

My father's engagement with the Royal Mint ceased at the end of the war.   By the terms of his contract, he was to have returned to London.   But he had made something of a reputation in Canada with some technical papers he had published on the metallurgical separation of platinum from gold, and on the establishment of a branch of the Royal Mint in South Africa.   He had come into personal contact with J. P. Bickell, a Canadian mining magnate, the owner of the famous McIntyre mine in the Porcupine district of Northern Ontario, and the Temiskaming silver mine near Cobalt. Bickell and his associates at this time were considering the purchase of the famous Dolly Varden mine in British Columbia.   My father was engaged by them to examine the Dolly Varden, and on his favourable report they not only began their negotiations for its purchase, but engaged him as its eventual manager.   Meanwhile they sent him to the Temiskaming mine in Cobalt, which, owing to the fall in the world price of silver, could no longer be worked profitably.   His task was to close it up and dispose of its assets to the best advantage. My father with his usual luck, and with that cleverness which made him an exceptional man, discovered a new rich vein of silver, and before it was closed two years later the mine paid its shareholders another $100,000 in dividends.

So, while the bud of life was beginning to open for me in Montreal, there was my father five hundred miles away in Northern Ontario, living in great comfort in the mine manager's house which he had taken over, enjoying himself in the local society of Haileybury, a summer resort on a lake ten miles away. While I relished the food of the Y.M.C.A. cafeteria after Charley's greasy platters, there was my father with the good Scots cook who had followed him from Ottawa, with a thoroughbred horse to ride in his leisure hours, and a new and interesting countryside to discover.

And there was I living in what seemed to me, too, great comfort, beginning to enjoy myself in the local society I found in the Drummond Street Y.M. and in a church hall to which I was invited to go and dance under the severe supervision of the nuns who ran it. There was I enjoying my freedom from domestic cares, breathing in great gulps of life with the thin, cold winter air of the St. Lawrence Valley.

Each morning I had breakfast in the cafeteria, then walked the few blocks to the office where we all, including Mr. Elliott, arrived at nine o'clock sharp. It was an excitement that for a time did not fail, to sit down each morning at my own desk, take out the files on which I was to work that day, and in the warmth of the steam-heated office immerse myself in the history of the Daubeny family, or lose myself in past investigations into the background of Mme Boileau, preparatory to going to call on them. Miss Bamford discussed the cases with me at first, but after a few weeks, when I had met them all several times, she only checked and countersigned the reports I wrote.

It did not take long in that intoxicating atmosphere for my head to spin alarmingly and my hand to tremble. I forget now how it began, whether in the course of my work or in my wanderings about the old city at nights or on Saturday and Sunday afternoons. Two of the friends I had made in the Y were handsome young

Americans who worked in the American Consul's office in Montreal. There was also living in the Y an elderly man who owned and managed himself a haberdasher's shop on the street-level of the Drummond Building. M. Bosanquet had lived all his life in Montreal. He was a French-Canadian and a Catholic, and a man of considerable taste and knowledge.

He began by taking the two American boys and me on Sunday afternoons to visit the old churches and convents in Montreal. M. Bosanquet seemed to be well known and liked by the heads of the different Orders and we generally ended up in the parlour of the Mother Superior, chatting and drinking tea. We then went to vespers. In those ancient and lovely churches my young soul, still bruised from my mother's death, responded with inarticulate ardour to the golden lights of innumerable candles, the smell of incense burning, the mysterious fall and rise of the voices of the choir.

Without my being aware of it at the time, M. Bosanquet noticed this. He began to take more interest in me than in the others. When I first noticed that he was inviting me, and excluding the others, I thought that he wanted to convert me to Catholicism. But he did not speak of this when he asked me to his room after dinner. He began to speak on other subjects which made me acutely embarrassed, and then he started to touch me which made me angry. I had never met a homosexual before, and this old man, who spent so much of his time in churches, and in the rooms of Mother Superiors, seemed to me suddenly horribly repulsive. I spent the rest of my time in Montreal avoiding him, but when I did see him in the dining-room sometimes, he only looked at me with his large

sad eyes, and I began to think I must have exaggerated
in memory what had happened. But I could not talk
to him without a feeling of repulsion, and soon he
ceased even to look at me.

It was the time when the soldiers were pouring back
from Europe. They came down the gangplank from
ship after ship, and the last discipline was when they
stood at attention outside their Regimental Headquarters while 'O Canada' was played; then they were
dismissed and were clasped by waiting arms; following
which, my duties became more arduous.

Their disbandment was bound to produce an uproar
in circles where lives were not lived with strict regularity, and for months I was busy plucking my charges
as brands from the burning. They were, of course,
inclined to misbehaviour; that is why they were in
the charge of our Department. The Armistice, all this
returning tide of virility, the excitement after the
monotony of leading strictly supervised lives, was too
much for the weaker among them; they slipped, and
it was my job to retrieve them. Since their fall from
grace usually took the form of sleeping with an unattached man, I frequently found myself, after every
evasion, form of bribery, and even seduction had been
used by my ward, up against a large and angry man
who, after trying to make me see eye to eye with him,
pushed his chest up against mine, and growled out — in
French it sounded worse — threats of what he would
do to me if I didn't mind my own fearful business. I
didn't much like those moments, but managed to hang

on grimly if silently while the woman, aware that her basic $480 annually was at stake, came back reluctantly to the side of respectability. I don't know how often during that spring and early summer of 1919 I was a witness to those dramatic scenes of renunciation.

Nor how often, as the summer wore on, I became a godfather. I must stand in that capacity to several score Montrealers, today no doubt men and women of nearly forty. I hail them across the decades that separate us since our last, and only meeting, which I remember but they will not. Not the particular day, nor the precise occasion; there was so little difference, if they do not mind my saying so, in the circumstances and the setting.

A warm summer's day, perhaps a very hot one, if it were July or August, when the heat in the St. Lawrence Valley can be oppressive and immense; a narrow street; a tenement we would call it in England; a pale priest climbing the narrow stairs ahead of me; an odour peculiar to these buildings in the lower town. It is difficult to describe its composition, it is a blend of so many things: cheese, garlic, stale wine, musty clothes, incense, floor or furniture polish; and superimposed on all these odours the unmistakable smell of church. But this might come from the priest, who also smells most definitely of feet; indeed, I cannot keep my eyes off his feet as he ascends the stairs ahead of me. I see his hairy ankles, the rough unpolished sandals he wears, the white skin with dark marks where the thongs have pressed, the ugly black stiff gown swirling about. He has hardly said a word to me since he met me down below. Does he suspect me of being the father? No, surely they had explained that I was the godfather.

And the apartment when we enter it, dark, the blinds drawn against the sun. One of the elements making up the compound smell is stronger here, as though we had reached a passage in a musical composition in which one instrument was allowed to express the theme authoritatively while the others kept up a subdued hum. There is no sign of a man except the priest and me, and neither of us is quite what you would call a man. An elderly figure opens the door to us; the girl's mother, perhaps more likely her aunt or grandmother, somebody who has taken charge. The airless little room into which we are shown. Sometimes one or two figures, inevitably in black, are discovered sitting silent and upright on chairs; they rise and bow as the priest comes in. He changes in front of us, produces his little portable font, someone brings the new-born babe from the mother's room. It comes, a little bundle smelling of poor babyhood, offering us the opportunity of breaking our *tableau vivant* with gestures wrung from us by its obbligato of misery played by a human voice but a few hours old, trying the air almost for the first time. The ceremony gets under way, and I add one more to the list of my godchildren. They are seventeen years younger than myself. I think, as I stand there, when I am thirty-five and settling down in life, this one will be eighteen — beginning, as I am now. It is hard to imagine that bundle in the shawl becoming a large man, or perhaps a pretty girl, capable in time of generating another such occasion as this. The nasal voice of the priest, speaking Latin with a Canadian accent, echoes in the lifeless air of the little room; I think to myself that with this one, little Alphonse or Jean-Jacques, whoever he is, I must try really to be a

godfather, look after him and help him if I can. But
within a week I will have forgotten him; it is impossible to admit to your heart everyone who comes
to it holding out his hands. I forgot these little mites
of misery because stronger and more silently persisting
attacks were being made on my emotions. Life, the
same spirit of life which fluttered weakly in them, the
pulse of which, beating in me, had brought me to this
stage, was now starting to throb, shaking my skinny
frame with its powerful beat.

On Sundays in the summer when the trees had
burst into life, I would walk with Gerry and George,
the two Americans, to the top of Mount Royal. There
we would sit and eat lunch at an open-air restaurant,
looking out over the city to the broad grey river in the
valley beneath and the green distances beyond. I liked
both these young men. Our talk was quite often of
girls, but it wasn't bad talk. The only girls we knew
were those we met at St. Joseph's Hall on Saturday
nights. They often unconsciously tempted us, but the
chaperones sitting in their nuns' habits along the wall
effectively prevented any intimacy from developing.
We held our partners stiffly off from us as we danced;
we were too unskilful to spare any thoughts for conversation; at the end of each dance we had to return
our partners to the benches against the wall, and go back
to our own benches on the opposite side of the room.
What then could we know of a woman, when we
could hold her at arms-length for such brief and arduous
moments ? Something, yes, something of which we

talked in subdued excited voices as we sat in the heat of the day at the top of the mountain.

After lunch we would walk along the mountain-top, eastwards and then westwards. The French society of Montreal paraded there in those days. We would glimpse something of the family life all three of us missed. But as we walked down the mountain-side through Westmount we could see into some of the large homes standing back only a few yards from the street, fronted by smooth green lawns which had sprung into beauty as suddenly as the trees. Three young men wearing straw hats, walking by these granite houses, pretending to be absorbed in each other's conversation, but eyeing with sidelong, envious glances the homes they would have loved to enter. Westmount was where the Scottish inhabitants of Montreal lived; house after house was inhabited by MacKays and McLeans and McDonnells, a fife and roll of drums of Scottish names. On the mountain-top we had watched the Beaubiens, the LaRousses and Le Viendriennes walking in solemn family conclave. When they descended from the mountain-top they went down by St. Lawrence Boulevard. They would never have driven down the winding avenues of Westmount, past those granite-faced houses, inhabited by descendants of families from Scotland. Any more than the McDonnells or the McLeans and the MacKays would have descended by way of St. Lawrence Boulevard, if on a Sunday afternoon they had taken an English visitor to see the view from the top of Mount Royal.

★

But these were glimpses of metropolitan Montreal vouchsafed to me only on Sunday afternoons. Here was a peculiar rivalry which had survived from the days, nearly two hundred years before, when Wolfe had conquered Quebec, and the English had taken Montreal. The city was cut into two as neatly as a knife can cut across a cake; to the east of St. Lawrence Boulevard the French Canadians, to the west of it the English Canadians. Different schools, different languages, different religions, kept the two as much apart as though a province separated them, not the width of a street. In business the two races had to mix, but they were very careful to keep their social lives quite distinct.

Nearly all my 'cases' were French; they were all, of course, poor. I wished that my duties might carry me into some of the granite-faced houses I saw in the winding avenues of Westmount, instead of up endless flights of stairs to cheap apartments, or to the ugly houses in the poorer suburbs of Montreal.

I had not seen Madame Daubeny for a long time. Soon after I took over her case, she disappeared from view. She was the one who was odd in the head. I must say that her appearance substantiated that reputation. Thin, pale, with washed-out staring eyes, with colourless hair screwed up into a bun, and clutching a dirty dressing-gown about her, she looked repellent when I first met her, and it was hard to believe that she was the mother of Jeanne and Marie-Pierre.

Monsieur Daubeny had been killed at Château-Thierry. The family appeared to be without relatives except some of M. Daubeny, who lived at Three Rivers and had renounced any interest in Mme Daubeny on the grounds that she had been a prostitute, and her daughters, now that she was no longer any good for the work, were engaged in the same trade. These scandalous charges had been investigated by my Department long before I came on the scene and had proved to be quite unfounded. What Mme Daubeny had been was not in question; she was now quite obviously a woman with a sick mind. Both the girls were employed in shops. What they did with their spare time was their own business, but they were in honest employment during the day, coming home to their mother at night.

But then, as I say, Mme Daubeny disappeared. I made several calls but was seen by either Jeanne or Marie-Pierre, received most warmly, made to drink a cup of coffee, was a little flirted with and made to feel rather gallant and amorous; and so ended by passing over to one of the girls the $15 I had brought with me. The receipt was signed by Jeanne or Marie-Pierre, who said their mother was in bed with a bad cold and couldn't be seen. This happened two or three weeks running. My suspicions should have been aroused, but I was by then so abandoned to a new excitement, or one new to me, that I deliberately shut my eyes to the danger signals that any good Administrative Clerk should have recognized.

In order that I shall not appear altogether a fool, I must say in my own defence that I had just reached an age when all that was vital and warm with life in me had surged up to bursting point, and longed to express itself in some emotional act. It was a year and a half since my mother had died. So much had happened in

that year; there had been so much deprivation, I had
been so often hungry, so frequently lonely, so much
deprived of privilege and freedom. And now the spring
had come, the days were lengthening, the earth was
warm and soft, the trees shuddered with life, and the
air after the long hard winter lay soft against one's
cheeks. I was in love with love; I needed only to
personalize it; and here in this plain little salon, with
the sun streaming in through the windows, I sat with
strong and unaccustomed tides flowing through my
heart while I watched these girls.

It was after a time as though they had drawn lots to
see who should be left with me, and Marie-Pierre began
to be alone there when I called. She explained that she
was taking her summer holidays from the shop, that
her mother had gone to visit her cousins at Three
Rivers to recuperate there from her severe attack of
influenza. If I would leave the money it would be
forwarded to her; her cousins would see that she
returned receipts for what she spent. It would be better
to leave the money for the month's pension; it was so
far to send it, each time it required a letter, each time
her mother had to be taken to the bank to cash a cheque.

This was against the regulations laid down for Mme
Daubeny, but instead of pointing that out, I abandoned
myself to the delicious tug of the tides sweeping through
me, and argued in an amorous sort of dispute with
the young girl, implying that only persuasion was
necessary to obtain my consent. She was more experienced than I was. She read my mind, and cheerfully
applied herself to my destruction; anything, I thought
bitterly afterwards, to get her hand on that money.
When next I called it was at eleven o'clock in the

morning. She opened the front door to me in her
nightdress. I could then have withdrawn, and reason
directed me to do it. But I could not swim against the
tides that were carrying me helplessly onwards into life,
and trembling and wordless I entered the flat as she
stood aside, holding the door for me.

I seemed in that never-to-be-forgotten summer unable to avoid these personal crises. Going over Mrs.
Cartier's accounts with her one afternoon, my mind
only half applied to the muddle she had produced, I
noticed suddenly for the first time the line of her jaw
and saw how delicate and soft was her skin. Surprised
by my own thoughts, I looked full at her, and the
whinnying protests with which she had been denying
that she had been extravagant died in the air, her grey
eyes grew large and she turned her head and looked at
me. It took a positive effort to return my own gaze to
the paper. She was silent for the rest of our interview,
answering my questions in low monosyllables, quite
unlike her usual voice. She accompanied me to the
door with downcast look; then in the dark hall suddenly threw her arms round my neck and kissed me
full on the lips. I was frightened in that embrace; I
did not know how to respond, I was repelled and attracted at the same time, but I wanted to get away. An
undignified scuffle followed before I was free and through
the door. Then her look of sadness smote me. What
could I do ? I could only seize her hand and squeeze it,
and smile at her in a foolish fashion. Then I was clatter-
ing down the stone stairs, hating myself for being what

I was; I thought, a sinner; I see now, after all these years, only a young man carrying his need for affection like a sandwichman his board, silently radiating a call that said, 'I want love, I want to be loved'.

But I could not find it anywhere, only, wherever I turned, those occasions that repelled me. Marie-Pierre, a prostitute; Mrs. Cartier, old enough to be my mother; the glacial girls of St. Joseph's Hall. Yet I could see that there was shining youth and beauty everywhere in this city. Sometimes, as I passed the Ritz Carlton Hotel on my way home, a group of lovely girls would come out. This was the time of short dresses and bobbed hair. Their beautiful legs would shine with silk, their bodies move with incredible grace. Going by I would see their warm skin, sometimes their laughing eyes, catch the faintest whiff of the scent they used and hear their tender girlish voices; and my desire for them as I walked by was overpowering. But there was no way in which I could know them. I longed desperately for a girl of my own age.

Mr. Elliott had been dangling before me for some time the prospect of my meeting his wife. ' You'll like her ', he would say; ' she always hits it off with young men your age. I'll fix it up with her and then give you the date.' Months passed, and no date was named, but the alluring prospect was referred to from time to time. 'Gee, we got to clear a date. I'd like you to come along and have dinner at the apartment with Mrs. Elliott and I; we'll just have a good chin together, eh? Kinda get acquainted a little more.' He beamed at me paternally, and I smiled back and said I looked forward to it; and I thought of my father, and his sardonic smile over having dinner with I.

Winter had passed into spring, and spring into early summer before the date was finally named. When it was, Mr. Elliott appeared the more excited of the two of us. Calling me into his office soon after he arrived one morning, he said to me, 'Say, look, are you doing anything tomorrow night? No? Good. We'd like you, Mrs. Elliott and I, to come along to the apartment for cocktails at six o'clock. We're going on to have dinner with some important friends, and we've been asked to bring someone to meet their niece. After dinner we're going to Westmount Hall for a dance. I guess you can dance all right, eh? I bet. Well, then, there we are. Got it fixed at last for you to meet Mrs. Elliott, and who knows, you might afterwards find a nice friend in this young girl we are introducing you to.'

I ardently hoped so. I bathed with great care, had a hair-cut and instructed the barber to lay my light and rebellious hair well down with brilliantine in honour of the occasion. Mr. Elliott himself opened the door to my punctual knock; like me, in blue suit, clean shirt and barbered hair, he had equipped himself for an evening in society, and like me he was very nervous. Mrs. Elliott rose to greet me. She was a thin, fair-haired woman of about forty, with a hard face and a voice that suggested she had a temper, and with enough good looks still to show that she must have been very pretty when she was younger, before her irritability became a habit not worth disguising. She treated me very much as though she were the boss's wife, which indeed she was, and I a boy from the office. This did not make me more nervous; rather less so. I sat silent while she talked and a wave of sympathy for Mr. Elliott swept over me. She must be frightening to live with.

While Mr. Elliott made his cocktail, trying to tell me with an air of pride and recklessness how he made his own gin, his wife droned out her little monologue with a torrent of refined chatter, and I looked about the room. It reminded me of the apartment we had had in Ottawa when my mother was dying; it was stuffy, shiny and uncomfortable-looking. What a bleak life, I thought, looking at my boss's bowed shoulders; what a life, Mrs. Elliott and this.

Mrs. Elliott was explaining who our host and hostess were, a Mr. and Mrs. Rogers. He was president of some company she spoke of with enormous respect. Mrs. Rogers and she were very, very close friends. Of course Mr. Rogers was quite out of the Elliotts' class as far as income went. Mr. Rogers, why, he was a member of the St. James's Club and the Rideau Club in Ottawa; and the family went to New York every November for their Christmas shopping and used to go to Europe for holidays before the war. Mr. and Mrs. Rogers knew England very well; we might find we had friends in common. Mr. Elliott had mentioned to her that my father worked in the Royal Mint; perhaps he knew Mr. Rogers.

But anyhow — she laughed loudly — it was a great honour to be invited to the Rogers'; they had simply thousands of friends. Of course Betty Rogers and she were very, very intimate friends. But it was nice of them to ask me to come too, didn't I think so ? I did think so, and said I hoped they wouldn't be disappointed when they met me. I heard myself utter a strangled little laugh at this sally. Mr. Elliott tried to support me by laughing too. But Mrs. Elliott quelled us both with a severe glance.

We sipped the Elliotts' home-made gin and orange juice. It wasn't at all bad; it sent a warm glow down my windpipe, and encouraged me to look Mrs. Elliott more boldly in the eye. I suppose her own windpipe was similarly warmed for some of the rigour of her posture melted, she sniffed, she allowed herself a weak, feminine smile. 'I don't know what I'll be saying if I drink too many of Sam's cocktails. You better watch yourself, young man. Well, well, I guess your mother doesn't even know you take a drink.'

'No,' I said, 'my mother is dead.'

Mrs. Elliott looked startled and a little of her natural tendency to choler crept back into her face. She looked at me severely, as though to say, 'Well, you might have told me. Springing it on me like that.'

I could not bear her, and looked away.

Mr. Elliott made hissing sounds of sympathy for me and reproof for his wife; it was exactly the same sound.

'Bad luck, boy,' he said. 'Too bad, too bad.'

'Is it a recent bereavement?' asked Mrs. Elliott. 'Did she pass away suddenly?'

'Eighteen months ago. No, she didn't die suddenly. I wish she had. She died very slowly and painfully. Of cancer.'

Mrs. Elliott clenched her hands together and sat forward in her chair.

'Poor boy,' she breathed. 'I suppose that was very tactless of me. But how was I to know? Samuel never tells me anything about his staff. I'm very sorry I stumbled on that subject. Now can I tell you something? I think you are brooding on it too much. You want to try and enjoy yourself. You are just entering on the best years of your life. I'm going to make it my business to see that you are taken out of yourself, and we'll start right tonight. You mix us another shot, Samuel, and don't you be too lavish with that orange juice, you old skinflint.'

Mrs. Elliott cried out with laughter as though to signal in a new mood. Mr. Elliott, with his mincing steps, went over to the tray, and soon we were drinking our seconds. I thought of the ice-breakers at Maisonneuve. They had thin noses like Mrs. Elliott; they rose majestically and as they sank, bit deeply into the ice that impeded them. Well, here's down the hatch, I thought, and felt my gullet flame again.

By the time we emerged from the Elliotts' apartment to drive to the Rogers' house, we were full of the party spirit. I saw now what Mr. Elliott had meant when he said she always hits it off with young men of my age. There was a warmth and sparkle about her, which hadn't been visible when I first met her, which brought out in me an unsuspected vein of humour. We jointly teased Mr. Elliott, who obviously enjoyed being the butt of our jokes; we treated him as a grave and reverend elder who was inclined to stop our fun. I forgot he was my boss, being carried away by the fire in my belly which had now spread to my head. I wasn't drunk, but I had got over my melancholy, and I was having a good giggle for the first time in a year or more.

I did not discover that night, or ever afterwards, what brought the Rogers and the Elliotts together in friendship. The Rogers lived in one of the big houses at the top of the mountain; Mr. Rogers was plainly a man of substance; his home showed it; his manner did; he had the granitic air of a successful business man.

He called the head of our office, now diminished in magnitude, Elliott *tout court*, while Mr. Elliott called him *Mr. Rogers*. The wives were Ethel and Betty to each other, but even between them, in spite of Mrs. Elliott's claims of intimacy, I sensed a barrier. I suspected that all three of us were there on some kind of sufferance, and I began to feel immensely sorry for the Elliotts and freezingly indifferent to the Rogers; and carried this ridiculous partisanship to a point where Mr. Elliott had to admonish me with a frown and a shake of his head.

Mr. Rogers served us a round of cocktails. Not in glasses now, but in little silver goblets taken straight from the ice and painful to hold. There was some liquid so icy to the teeth that it made the nerves jump, and almost simultaneously so fiery to the stomach that it sent shivers down the insides of my legs and up my spine. At the same time, fatally, my self-confidence was restored. O! lamentable moment, when the shivers start and restraint is laid aside like a garment.

The girl who was of the party I had hardly noticed at first, so absorbed had I been in the relationship between the Elliotts and the Rogers, but when we went into dinner and I found myself sitting beside her, I suddenly noticed that she was very pretty. Violet was her name; her eyes were wide apart and clear, her nose short, her skin very delicately coloured; she smiled a great deal and said very little.

The victim of shivers, I was not at my brightest, but I was at my rashest. My desire was to say something startling that would rivet everyone's attention, which would level up the Elliotts to the Rogers. I had been all for bursting in on the general conversation when the move to the dining-room was made, and I suddenly found myself sitting beside Violet. My aggressive instincts subsided, and what I then did not recognize as my amorous ones took command. I found myself able to talk to her unselfconsciously, and I began to enjoy myself.

But soon embarrassment overwhelmed me. I heard Mrs. Elliott telling Mrs. Rogers about my mother's death in the 'poor boy' vein which I hated so much. I pretended to take no notice but it was impossible not to overhear, and not to feel exasperated with this woman who was my boss's wife. I glared at her, trying to put into my expression all the dislike that I felt. She smiled sweetly and sadly at me in return, and I began to think with displeasure of the long evening ahead.

After dinner we got into two cars, I managing by a certain amount of agility to get into the Rogers' back seat next to Violet. We drove to a large hall where an orchestra was assembled on a raised dais, and parties sat at tables round the room. My first dance was with Violet. All that I knew of dancing I had learnt at St. Joseph's; the general idea was to hold your partner at practically arm's length and push her rapidly in the direction you were going. The one-step was nothing but a fast walk; the fox-trot could be even faster because then you did little two-steps at the turn and waggled your hips a bit as the music smote you. The waltz was a delirious sort of whirl in which — at the stage at which I was — you muttered to yourself 'one-two-three, one-two-three' and thought with agony of what you had to do when you turned.

Violet saw that I was a primitive, I suppose. We

had not gone half the length of the room before she smiled at me, got in beneath my St. Joseph's guard, and put her cheek next to mine. The effect was electrifying. I was saved only from measuring my length on the floor by her acting as a prop. I must have broken into profuse perspiration, but I remembered for years afterwards the fragrance of this girl, her delicious softness, the light sunny smell of her hair. At one bound I had made it to paradise. This was what I had dreamed of when I thought of girls, this sweet determination, this unhesitating surrender, this soft compassion. I was suddenly head over heels in love and dancing with some sense of rhythm where a few moments before I had been tense and watchful, engaged in brisk physical exercise.

Puffing with glory I moved with Violet at the end of the dance to the two tables where our little party had congregated. Others came up and spoke to the Rogers, Mr. Elliott was looking about the room with a calculating eye, but Mrs. Elliott stared at me with a fixed and frightening smile, and I felt some of the confidence run out of me. She said something to the effect that I was quite a dancer. I made the conventional protest but said I hoped she would honour me with the next and try it out for herself. She said she would, but shook her head a little sadly, saying it was hard I should have to dance with an old married woman when there were so many young pretty girls about. I should have protested against this self-disparagement, and when I didn't, her smile deepened, but not in pleasure.

The glory had departed when I got to the floor a second time. Mrs. Elliott had a grip like iron; I felt like a colt which has just been broken and is in shafts

for the first time. She determinedly led, I woodenly
followed. We moved in our hostile embrace round the
room, talking most of the time as though we were old
friends just met who had a great deal to say to each
other. She asked me about my home and family, and
then told me about her own. She came from London,
Ontario; her father was an outstanding lawyer there;
he had had the first automobile ever seen in London;
they had done a lot of entertaining; she had travelled
a great deal with her parents, been to New York quite
often, had been to Chicago and Los Angeles. It had
been strange to settle down as a married woman after
all that excitement, she guessed. Mr. Elliott had been
the last man her parents had expected her to marry, but
she had always been one for doing the unexpected
thing. She hated being conventional, she guessed; it
just bored her dreadfully.

Mrs. Elliott was what in our family we had always
called an 'autobob'. Steered by her, we moved at a
majestic pace around the room, and while my ears
were assailed by her life story I watched out for Violet,
glimpsing her now and then in the arms of a good-
looking man with a small black moustache and an air
of smiling self-confidence. Once, as she swept past,
she smiled at me over his shoulder, and I felt suddenly
dizzy with rapture. When the dance ended I hurried
Mrs. Elliott to our table. 'Why, I do believe,' she said
with an angry laugh, 'he wants to get rid of me. I
guess he's got his eye on someone else. I guess I can
take a hint all right.'

I could with great pleasure and satisfaction have
choked her. I thought that everyone around must have
heard her and must know that she was referring to my

feelings for Violet. I thought how sickening it was that I should be betrayed in this fashion by this addle-pated woman, and I wondered that Mr. Elliott had managed to refrain from the daily, the hourly temptation to murder her. My face burned with embarrassment and my ears rang, but when I recovered a little I found that no one had paid much attention to what Mrs. Elliott had said. Violet was talking to the man with the black moustache. She smiled at me again, and I got up and went and stood beside her. When the music started again I did not ask her to dance. I put my hand timidly on her arm. She looked up, smiled, rose, and we were away, once more settling in what was to me a warm embrace.

Later in the evening we stood near the door waiting for an encore. 'It's hot in here,' she said. 'Let's walk up and down the street.'

The hall stood on one of the steep-winding roads which climbed to the top of the mountain. All the cars were parked with their front wheels turned in to the kerb. It was steep walking uphill, and when we turned to walk down again it was almost as difficult to balance against the descending pathway. 'No place for a girl with high heels,' she said. The lights of the lower town swam in the valley beneath us. It was wonderfully isolated, wonderfully cool where we were on the cliffs high up above that diamond-studded sea. It was a long time since I had felt so happy.

She stumbled, and I took her arm. I had never held a girl this close before. It hurt like a pain suddenly until she put her face up to mine and brushed my cheek with her lips. The hurt dissolved then in a flood of feeling, and suddenly the shackles of my boyhood fell from me with an almost audible clang as I touched a girl's lips with love for the first time in my life.

The direction of my life turned a little. No longer were my Sundays spent walking with Gerry and George and my Saturday nights at St. Joseph's Hall. Almost overnight I found myself plunged into social activity of two quite different kinds. Violet invited me to lunch on the Sunday following the dance in order to meet her parents. They lived a little way out of Montreal in a very pretty house with a most attractive garden, one of a number of houses in a community attached to a golf club. At the same time, through Gerry and George I met Housie Morris, a one-armed veteran of the war, fat, pink, ugly and cheerful, who lived with his new and handsome blonde wife in an apartment-house near the office. Housie was to teach me something that I was never to forget, poker, and quite unconsciously was to affect me at a distant turning-point in my life. He was the most vulgar, loud-mouthed, affable, good-hearted fellow I had ever met; in fact, I had never encountered anyone like him before. He kept me constantly surprised. 'Jeez, kid, take your peepers off me, will you?' I can see him now, about to deal, with his thumb holding the pack in his one large hand, and raising protuberant black eyes to me. I see him sitting in his undershirt, he always stripped down to that to play; I see him managing the game with eyes constantly on the move, reminding those who had not put up their ante, laying down a judgment in the post-mortem that generally followed a hand,

instructing a tyro like myself, making change and entering loans and sales on a grubby piece of paper, eating a
sandwich, calling for beer, telling a story; tireless,
never angry, the energizer of the party.

Every Saturday the 'game' was on. Housie was a
born gambler, and had got his nickname from running
Russian Bank in his battalion in France. We all finished
work at one o'clock on Saturday. The game started
an hour later at two, went on all that day and all that
night, finishing up at breakfast-time on Sunday morning. There was a running supply of sandwiches and
ice-cold beer for which no charge was made on the
individual, but in payment for which Housie was
allowed to take ten cents from each pot. Since we
played something like twenty pots an hour, and kept
up our rounds for nineteen hours, it can be seen that
Housie made a good thing out of his hostmanship.
But nobody minded; the winner always paid. No
one, of course, could sit at a poker table for eighteen or
twenty hours without respite. Two horsehair sofas
stood in the room. At any moment, if luck was
running against one, if sleep was not to be withstood,
one could withdraw from the game, fling oneself on
the sofa, fall asleep to the sound of voices and the click
of chips, and wake refreshed to stagger back to the
table. Only Housie never slept; nothing could bend
him, not fatigue, or bad luck or boredom; nothing
except nine o'clock on Sunday morning when he smelt
coffee coming from the kitchen, and heard his wife
slopping about in her slippers on the kitchen floor.
Then he would look round at our pallid faces. 'Well,
fellers,' he would say, slapping the pack. 'Last round,
eh?' And off we would go, the amateurs amongst us

desperately doubling our bets to try to recover our losses.

We lost sometimes more than we could afford, which meant going hungry the following week. We won sometimes, which gave us happiness out of all proportion to the size of our winnings. The game was strictly honest, Housie saw to that. But the session had a special value for me. It taught me self-control, which was a lesson I needed to learn, and it taught me something about human nature. I was quick to learn; I had to be, for no mercy was shown. Out of those all-night sessions I learnt, not how to make money gambling, but how to lose as little as possible when it is necessary to lose, and how to extract as much as possible from a winning streak. Since the chances of life that are not within our control often respond to the same treatment, I reckon that I learnt at Housie's table one of the most valuable lessons of my life.

I should have played every Saturday if it had not been for Violet, and had it not been for Mrs. Elliott who, since the night of the dance, had constituted herself my social guardian. I enjoyed my visits to Violet's home. Her father was a banker of some sort, a well-to-do man, and her mother was as pretty as Violet and very youthful-looking even in my young eyes. Violet was their only child, and they were so intent on having a good time themselves that without realizing it they neglected her. They allowed her to do what she liked within reason, and left her completely unchaperoned in this big house. Often we found ourselves in our youthful love-making carried to the edge of an emotional precipice over which it would have been only too easy to fling ourselves. What saved us was not the love we

M

pretended to feel for each other but an inexplicable sadness each of us felt for the plight of the other. She thought of me as almost an orphan, unloved and unwanted, a waif cast upon the world. Remembering my own happy home and the way we all lived each other's business, I felt a sadness for her isolation. She seemed to me as lonely as a cloud. But I loved her truly, sweet Violet that she was, and my love lasted several months until it was swamped by an opposing tide.

I went to the Elliotts' several times. Having been accepted, alas, I was bidden to attend any occasion on which the Elliotts entertained if there was an extra lady for whom nobody could be found, or if Mrs. Elliott required to impress someone with her motherliness. I don't know which occasion I dreaded most; the first, which often left me partner to someone old enough to be my aunt; or the second, when Mrs. Elliott spoke in whispers of the 'poor boy who had lost his mother', 'like a son to Sam and I, never having been blessed in that way'. I think on the whole I preferred the maiden aunt nights.

Mr. Elliott now called me at the office by my Christian name; Miss Bamford remarked several times that I looked tired, and wondered aloud if I were not staying up too late at night; and my charges, who once had regarded me with suspicion, now started to complain when I missed a visit, and thought that I was neglecting them and paying more attention somewhere else. My summer holiday was approaching and I was longing for it. I had arranged to go and stay with my father at Temiskaming. I hadn't seen him for over a year, and I had never been to Northern Ontario. I was tired, stale and uneasy in spirit.

On a hot night in August I left Montreal. I had a sleeping-berth, and I awoke in the morning as we were skirting the shores of Lake Nipissing. This was my first view of the North. The train rode steadily among the outcroppings of rock, the summer sun shone from a faultless sky on the blue waters of the lake. Not a house to be seen, no farms, no animals, no roads; only the wilderness of bush and rock and water stretching to the horizon.

At North Bay the Canadian National became the Temiskaming and Northern Ontario Railway. No change in the landscape, but the track turned sharply north, leaving the transcontinental line flinging itself to the west. Turned north, and ran beside further lakes, and the rocks pressed in and became higher, and the railway squeezed itself painfully between narrow clefts and inched its way towards the Arctic. Some time after lunch we slid into Cobalt. A plateau opened out, and there were the mine chimneys, and, when the train stopped, the old sound of the mill stamps. Even more familiar, there was my father, looking as smart and well-tailored as ever, in the accustomed riding-breeches and polished riding-boots; standing there benignly, his head turned to hide his bad eye, smiling and watching me critically as I advanced. How well I knew that parental stance. By now I could pronounce what was running in his mind. Changed? Galoot-ish? Those shoes! Cake-cutters! What's he know of life? I wish he wouldn't wear his hat so far back on his head. Then the smile would signify that he recognized I was his son, and he would move. 'Hello, son. I'm so glad to see you.'

In the Gray-Dort outside the station was Clive,

looking at me out of his innocent blue eyes curiously. I had hardly seen him since Mother's death; he had grown a little, he was now fourteen. But he was the same Clive, blond, quiet, serene, where the rest of us were tense and brittle.

The Temiskaming mine lay five miles to the east of Cobalt, the farthest out of the mines. The Gray-Dort silently sped along a firm road cut between rock, passing various mines which my father named to me. We came at last to the Temiskaming, no different from the scores of mines we had known in our lives, the Leonora, the Lawlers, the Mount Sir Samuel in Australia; the Giant and the Cam and Motor in South Africa. There was the mine-shaft and the hoist-house, the assay office and the Company office, the men's bunkhouse, and the house of the Chief himself, distinguished as always, even during a temporary occupation like this, by a garden and a lawn.

It was lovely to come home again, and to be lapped in comfort. It did not strike me as odd that my father should be living in luxury like this while I lived in a room in a Y.M.C.A.; that he should be driving an expensive car, keep several riding horses, have all that he wanted to eat and drink while I went often hungry. He had always had the best; none of us had ever questioned his extravagances; they were a part of the apparatus that had always gone and would always go with him. He was unique.

He treated me as an honoured guest, but beyond a polite enquiry as to whether I liked my job he asked nothing about my life in Montreal. It was his form of politeness, or perhaps it was his way of implying 'I am in no position to criticize anyone's way of life, so tell

me nothing which might force me to become hypo-
critical in condemning you for doing it'.

I think he loved me as I loved him. We had exactly
the same interests; we loved horses and dogs, and we
loved books, and we were never tired of talking of
them. After I had been there a week he said it was a
pity I had to return to Montreal so soon, and he asked
whether my job was likely to lead to anything. I said
I doubted it, and he asked whether I had thought what
I meant to do with my life. I honestly could not
answer. I had no plans except to keep alive, to do
which it was necessary to work, so the simple motive
of my life was to try to keep a job. My father said,
'Would you like to be a Mining Engineer? There is a
School of Mines at Haileybury. You could live here
with me and go over to it each day. I don't know how
we would manage in the winter. Perhaps you could
stay with friends of mine in Haileybury, and come
home at week-ends.'

The young engineer of the mine, an American from
Michigan named Harry Sparks, was living with us in
the house at Temiskaming. He treated my father as
though he were his own and me as though I were a
prodigal brother who had returned from wickedness.
He was present at this conversation, and he broke in
like an evangelist rousing the apathetic to the chance of
glory. 'It's a wonderful life,' he said, 'and we have
lots of fun here. Besides this northern country is just
on the edge of the greatest development. The gold-
fields in the Porcupine District are going to become the
most famous in the world. Isn't that so, Chief? Look
at the McIntyre. Look at the Hollinger. In the whole
history of mining there has never been a time more

promising for a young fellow going into it.'

My father, without trying to persuade me too hard, flattered me by his interest into deciding that I would do this.   Harry Spark's enthusiasm was a spur, and my own sensual appreciation of the pleasures of home was the final factor.   I never seriously asked myself whether I was interested in mining, whether I had even in embryo the qualities that would go to make a good engineer.

But it was all settled that I should start in at the Haileybury School of Mines in September, and I was to return to Montreal only to give two weeks' notice before coming back to Cobalt.   I did not think that my departure from the office would make any difference to anyone;   I occupied a very humble post, which could be quickly filled again by someone without experience. I wrote to Mr. Elliott from Cobalt telling him my plans, and saying that I would be back in the office on August 16th to work out my notice.

No answer came, but Mr. Elliott called me to his room on the first morning of my return.   He looked sombre;   he acted towards me as though he knew he should know me, but for the minute had forgotten who I was.

'Gee, feller, have you got to add to my troubles?' was his greeting.   'Sit down, sit down.   Quitting, heh?   Well, I can't stop you.   It's inconvenient.   We've trained you;   now you run off to do something else, we've got to go back to the starting-point and begin again.   Still, it's a free country.   But what happened to you you made up your mind so quickly?   You've been working here less than a year and you take a full summer's vacation, the understanding being that you will go on. I could withhold a week of your final salary, but I'm not going to do it. I tell you, it's a free country.' There was a definite pause. 'For most people,' he added.

I hadn't really been listening to what he was saying. From the moment I walked into the room and saw his haggard looks, from the moment he spoke of adding to his troubles to this final poignant phrase, I had been trying to imagine what was wrong.

'Is Mrs. Elliott all right?' I asked him.

He looked at me sharply.

'You want to do me a favour? You come up some time before you leave and say goodbye to her. She took a fancy to you, young feller, and she doesn't feel so good about your walking out like this. She doesn't give her friendship easily. When she does, and the other party just walks out, it isn't so good. No siree, it isn't so good.'

I don't know why, but a nasty feeling of guilt began to spread over me. I had not thought I was being inconsiderate in leaving, but suddenly I began to feel as though I were disliked and it left me very uncomfortable.

From the others I parted on much happier terms. I went to Housie Morris's for a final night of poker, dropped twelve dollars which I could ill afford, and listened to a flood of sage advice from Housie. I said goodbye to my various charges. None of them showed much surprise or feeling. Cobalt was a fabled place far off in the Northern wilderness; I had made no impact on their lives, but they in a hundred soft impressions, hardly realized at the time, had left little marks on my character, never to be effaced.

I took an evening to say goodbye to Violet. We had known each other only for three months, and in that time had discovered very little about each other. My feelings for her were rather more proprietorial than loving; I was proud to have for the first time someone whom I could call my girl. I see now that Violet provided a channel for all my mixed and fluttering adolescent yearnings, and gave me in an innocent way some small foretastes of bliss. But I loved her chiefly because I was the object of her loving thoughts; such delusions help to give substance to the good opinion young men strive to hold of themselves.

And now that I was to say goodbye all this unreality started to vanish, for her as well as for me. The image we each had of the other as the loved and the loving one began to fade, and in its place the reality coldly emerged, a shy awkward young man saying goodbye to a young girl whose attention was already roving purposefully amongst the men she knew, wondering who would take his place.

There remained only my interview with Mrs. Elliott, and I put it off as long as I could. In my last week at the office I telephoned her from the little cafeteria where I often ate. I said that she had probably heard from her husband that I was going home to pursue my education — oh, pompous phrase! — and I wondered if I might call to say goodbye.

My chattering voice, high-pitched as always when I am nervous, echoes in my inner ear after all these years. And so do Mrs. Elliott's cold, distant, monosyllabics, pregnant with doom. Mrs. Elliott said yes, she said yes, she said nothing more. I asked when I might come, and she said it did not matter, and she said yes, I had better come the next evening after the office. They were going out, but she supposed that I would not be staying long.

I emerged from that 'phone booth with damp hands, a thudding heart and a pronounced feeling of guilt. That was Mrs. Elliott for you; she was certainly a strong personality. I had done nothing wrong, but I had to keep telling myself so.

The next evening I gave Mr. Elliott half an hour's start and then took a street-car to their apartment. I had bought half a dozen red roses, I had rehearsed a little speech, and I had got myself into such a state that when Mr. Elliott opened the door to me I handed him the roses. He entered the drawing-room ahead of me, passed the flowers to Mrs. Elliott and said, 'He brought you some flowers,' wonderingly, as though there had been something terribly astute in that move.

Mrs. Elliott did not deign to smell them or to unwrap them from their transparent paper. She inclined her head towards me and said, 'Won't you take a seat?' There was no sign of Mr. Elliott's gin; the interview, for that was how I thought of it now, was to be brief and not lubricated by Mr. Elliott's home-made aid to good fellowship, so much a feature of my first visit here.

Mrs. Elliott asked me about my holiday, not, as I quickly discovered, out of genuine interest but in order to bring us to the point from which she proposed to swoop on me; the fact that I had used this as an opportunity to rearrange my life in a way that would take me out of her range of influence.

She said that she had been very surprised to hear from Mr. Elliott of what I had decided to do; she couldn't help feeling that Mr. Elliott had been badly treated in not having a hint earlier of my intentions. I said with eager clamour that I'd never thought of the idea until my father put it to me while I was on holiday. As I spoke I felt, as I'm sure she intended, a rush of guilt. Had I decided rather too quickly? Should I have given him longer notice? I honestly had not thought that my going would make much difference to the organization. I was not much more than an office-boy, certainly the most junior member of the staff.

'I don't know what sort of a mining engineer you'll make,' she said, 'if you stick it long enough to become one. I suspect you're rather inclined not to stick to things. It's a little fault you should try to get over. It lets other people down so badly. Of course you're young, and you may change. But I think it's always a good thing to size up one's weaknesses and try to remedy them as one goes along.

'If you hadn't lost your mother, you might be turning out quite differently. My hope was that I might in some small way have tried to take her place. You need a little guiding, if you don't mind my saying so. In time you might turn out quite a good man, given that there is someone to steer you along the right course. Well, I've had that opportunity taken away from me, and I'm sorry. Sorry for you, I mean, because it wouldn't have been an easy or pleasant task for me; it would have been something I would have undertaken as a duty, because you have lost your own mother.

'You won't mind my saying it, will you, but I hope you will try to get over what I suspect is a little vanity about yourself. You know what I mean? Just the teeniest bit of self-satisfaction shows now and then in your face and manner. It isn't very becoming. Of course I know young men living on their own, away from home, are inclined to get spoilt. I suppose it isn't surprising, especially since the war, when all the good old standards have been lowered. But really you haven't got an awful lot to be self-satisfied about yet, have you? You aren't good-looking, and you certainly haven't started to make your mark in life. I'd just watch that, if I were you. One day I think you'll thank me for having been frank with you.'

I licked my dry lips and looked sideways at Mr. Elliott. I don't know what I expected to find, a swift glance of sympathy or a downcast look of shame at a wife who went on like this. I didn't expect what I did find, Mr. Elliott gazing at his wife with quite a rapt look. He really seemed to appreciate what she was saying.

As for me, there was beginning a roaring in my ears as little waves of anger mounted in me. I thought, if I get to my feet my legs will tremble; if I speak my voice will come out a squeak. I must get out of here.

I stood up and said, 'Thank you very much,' and put out my hand to her. I shouted goodbye, and pushed past Mr. Elliott to the door. I heard him stumbling after me, but I grabbed my hat and hurried through the door, slamming it behind me. I did not wait for the elevator, but ran down the stairway, my eyes stinging, my heart choked with anger.

On my last afternoon in Montreal I rode out to Maisonneuve, and walked round the grey untidy streets where I had come less than a year before in Mac's company. I meant to spend that last afternoon nostalgically. I wanted to retrace my steps and remember all that had happened to me in this year. I was in a state of remorse, and I was anxious to exhume my immediate past and analyse it. Ever since my interview with Mrs. Elliott two nights before I had been feeling very melancholy. Running out of the room as I had done, allowing myself to get angry and rude, seemed to bear out what Mrs. Elliott had said : I was vain, I could not bear to be corrected, I was unreliable, I was spoilt. All that it would have made my mother sad to find in me I had in the two years since her death become. Where had I gone wrong ? Was the freedom to do what I liked too intoxicating for me ? Did I have a weak head for life ? Was I wicked ?

I thought then that I was ; the image of my mother's face looked at me through my mind in bewilderment and pity, and I hated myself that I could not return her sad and searching gaze without in imagination dropping my eyes in shame. The consciousness of wrong-doing is as vivid as a sharp pain to a sensitive, growing boy, and the pain is the sharper when he bears it alone. In a year I had made no friend to whom I could talk about myself. That was significant too. I had not been to Communion in all the year I had been here. I had promised my mother before she died that I would go at least three times a year, and every month if possible. Instead I had been to a few services at the Catholic churches, but as a sightseer dropping in to stare, not as a communicant emptying his soul of its sin and receiving the healing balm of the sacraments.

I had seen Mac only twice since I had moved down to Drummond Street, and each time he had looked me up. I had never been to see him. Walking now along the street that bordered the mile-long wall of Vickers', I wondered if he were inside, or whether he was on night shift and now asleep in that horrible bed at Mme Boucher's. I half thought of going there to look him up, but I was too desolate to want human company.

There were the iron gates where we had waited that first day in October; there was the works office and the policeman standing by. Behind the tall barrier the lofty chimneys threw their smoke into the sky. In the street there was comparative silence, and there was I. Only a hundred feet away behind this wall the grim, staccato, unceasing chatter of work would be vibrating the wooden planks that formed the rough floor every-where. Two thousand men would be at their jobs in holds, on decks, under the great bellies of the ships. If I had not left them I would have been there too, in greasy overalls, with face blackened by the coke fires in which we heated the rivets, un-singular, unambitious, anonymous.

That was the trouble. I had wanted to get on. Something had been restless in me ever since I had been about eleven or twelve, drawing me on to try to dis-tinguish myself. It had been the cause of all the un-happiness in my life; my happiness lay with the herd of my fellow-men and I ought never to leave them.

I promised myself as I stepped on a street-car to get back to the centre of Montreal that I would remember this, and the next time the ambition came over me to try to excel I would shrug it away. Friends meant more than anything on earth.

CHAPTER EIGHT

LIVING in comfortable surroundings, under no necessity to earn my keep, I should now have been happy, but I was not. I had no money worries any longer. My father as always gave me no regular allowance, but he seemed to take a favourable view of me, and whenever I asked him for a little money for a special purpose, he gave it to me. He spent money on me as he had always done on his extravagances, like cigars and whisky and good clothes. He suddenly took a whim to be indulgent towards me as a son; he did not spend much on me, but the little he spent gave him a feeling of fond indulgence. I was sharp enough to notice this, but was careful not to overplay the situation.

He put at my disposal an old car, an ancient Briscoe, which I drove backwards and forwards to the school until the snow came, which put the car out of action for the winter. I trained a St. Bernard dog we had to pull me on the sleigh. His progress was erratic, but on the whole he accomplished his purpose, though not without long pauses, when he stood panting heavily and wagging his great tail, while I exhorted him with cries of 'Mush! Mush!' to proceed. He got me, or I got him: together we got to where the street-car line began. I would put Barney in a stable and ride the street-car into Haileybury.

I was not being a success at the School of Mines, but

I kept this news from my father. As I had uneasily suspected before I began, I had a blind spot for all scientific knowledge. At school chemistry had been absolute hell. Blinding headaches would come upon me at Berkhamsted in the afternoons when we were supposed to be in the Labs. So strong was this antipathy that I would have a bilious attack and would vomit, and be sent back to the house to lie down. Mineralogy now affected me as chemistry had done then. I simply could not stretch my mind to understand what they were saying. Trigonometry was as bad, and other mathematics were only a degree less worse. I was as backward and as dense as an idiot, and my utter incapacity soon attracted the attention of the Principal. I had some ominous interviews. It was made clear to me that soon my father must be consulted, and that the authorities were considering recommending my retirement. I felt a plunge of fear. Nobody likes to fail. I thought, Father will be shocked, I will have disgraced him; and found to my utter surprise no feeling of contrition, though the fear was there. Would he be shocked? Would he be even interested?

Some strange changes had come over our way of life since the unhappy days at the time of my mother's death. They had come over the whole world, but the contrast was stronger in our family. Prohibition had become law, and cocktails and drinks which had formerly been taken in careful measure were now served at every party, and even when there was no party. Dancing had become a craze, and everyone danced before lunch and dinner and even during courses — not only young people, but old people too. The relief from years of war strain affected everyone, and since everyone bought whisky from bootleggers, and drank too much, and gambled, and engaged in love affairs, no one felt free enough himself from blame to adopt a reproving attitude towards anyone else. I had my father on that point, and despised myself for recognizing it. No doubt he despised himself because he could no longer control me. I was preparing myself for failure, and he must have known it as much as I did. But communication of the old kind between us was broken, and I wished, and perhaps he did too, that it might not have been so.

When the Principal told me that unless I did well enough in the spring exams, he could not allow me to come back to the school, I did not tell my father this. I said only that I hated the place and was getting nowhere, and that I wanted to leave.

'And what are you going to do?' my father asked.

Get some practical experience, I replied. I said I wanted to work underground. Then I would know if I wanted to be a mining engineer.

He said: 'It might not be a bad idea. For a few months, at any rate. I worked when I was your age. Try it out, anyhow, and see. I'll put you with Joe Sweet.'

Joe Sweet had worked in the Cobalt mines for twenty years. He was a reliable, top-grade miner, a driller who got bonus pay for working on paying veins. Pink-cheeked, smooth-faced, always wearing a clean shirt and freshly-washed overalls, he was turned out by Mrs. Sweet for work every day in spick-and-span condition. He chewed tobacco constantly, smoking being forbidden in the mine, and interrupted his flow of talk, which was otherwise unceasing, only to spit. He

N

regarded me with friendly, smiling eyes, but his opinion of my capacities was very low, and he did not hesitate to voice it, though always with a slow humorous drawl.

'I'll be god-damned if I ever see such an awkward bastard — heh, heh,' he would chuckle. 'If you can get yourself backed-up, arse to, and the hose twisted, you will,' he would say. 'Good job your Dad's the boss : you wouldn't last five minutes but for that, heh, heh,' and a stream of brown juice would shoot past my face and splash on the rock.

The trouble was that I was fascinated with the scene. We were 1500 feet underground. We made our way along narrow passages which every now and then opened into great caverns of solid rock. The lamps we wore in our caps or at our breasts would light up the steep, shining walls and be lost in the darkness above. Sometimes Joe would show me the silver veins, shining and glinting in the light of our lamps. The silence was of the tomb until I had connected the hose to the air-pipes running along the passages. Then the rattle of Joe's drill would shatter the dark, oppressive air. He would drill half a dozen holes, we would put in sticks of dynamite, and then withdraw along the passage. A few minutes later there would be a tremendous shaking roar, and the sound of rock tumbling and the smell of cordite in the air. We would pick our way back over the fallen rock, and sometimes Joe's lamp, running enquiringly up and down the raw face, would light on a vein of silver, exposed for the first time since it had been folded away a million years before in some roaring cataclysm of this rocky earth. My heart thudded, my mind wondered at it, and absorbed in thought I would do the wrong thing, or nothing when I was supposed to be doing something with my hose, and Joe would emit a stream of tobacco juice, and say, 'If ever I see a more forgetful son of a bitch. . . .'

When the cage swung us up to the surface at night, I seemed to come not into another world, but into another dimension. I found it hard to breathe the surface air after eight hours underground. Stepping off the cage, I would feel giddy, and sometimes stumble, and when I stood beneath the shower in the shower-house I would feel waves of faintness and nausea sweep over me until I had to put my hands flat against the walls to support myself. I did not know what was wrong with me, but when I got back to the house after bathing I felt so unutterably weary that I could only stagger to my bed and fall on it, and lie in a half-doze until the bell summoned me to dinner.

One evening, as I returned from the bath-house to our own house, one of these waves of blackness which seemed to come up from the ground, reach almost to my neck and then generally recede, leaving me giddy and breathless, did not recede: it swept over me as a wave does in the surf, and I felt the hard gravel prick my face as I fell on it, and then a dull pain at the base of my head for the moment before oblivion wiped out all feeling.

When I came to I was lying on my bed and my father was bent anxiously over me. 'Don't move, old son. Dr. Smith is coming out. Drink this.' He poured a tablespoonful of brandy. I had to lift my head to drink it. It went down the wrong way and I coughed and spluttered, and felt it dribbling down my chin. The pain came back like the blow of a heavy hammer, and to add to the general downpour I could feel the tears gush from my eyes. I was so weak that I could do nothing but sob. Besides this, I thought, would prevent my father from making me move again. I wanted only to lie still until this weakness or this pain retreated.

Old Dr. Smith arrived, and put the damp cigar from which he rarely allowed himself to be separated on my dressing-table, opened his old bag and took out his stethoscope. He sounded my chest, glaring the while at me from under his bushy eyebrows. Then he glared at my father. 'What's this boy been doing?' he demanded. He tapped a couple of enormous pills from a bottle in his bag, made me swallow them, and said to my father, 'Come out with me while I telephone. We'll get an ambulance and put him into hospital.'

An hour later I was in Cobalt Hospital, and there I remained for three months. My father, all contrition now, got a specialist up from Toronto to examine me and confirm old Dr. Smith's opinion. I had heart disease. An enlarged heart had affected the valves, and for a little while I was thought to be dangerously ill. For a week or two I lay there thinking of death, and then the blackness lifted, and the tide of life flowed back into my thin body. I could feel it, the very stream of life running through my parched veins. But I was not allowed to move. Day after day I lay there, and the piles of books which my family kept bringing me mounted higher and higher about my bed. I read until my eyes were almost starting from my head, and the hours, which otherwise might have dragged, fled by.

★

When I came out of hospital it was quite clear that I could never do heavy work again, and once more I dreamt of the possibility of working for a newspaper or a magazine. But I had no experience and no introductions, and I did not know how to begin to go about finding such a job. While I was convalescing at home, Jack Bickell came on a visit to the mine. He talked to me from time to time, and knowing that he was a rich and influential man, I exercised all the charm and intelligence I had at command — and it wasn't much — to earn his interest and help. Miraculously it worked. He was President of Paramount Pictures Corporation in Canada. He said he would speak to the General Manager. A few days later I got a letter from Paramount offering me a job in their sales department at $25 a week, commencing immediately, and I left for Toronto, feeling that at last I was to get a foothold in the world of imagination and art.

I little guessed what was in store for me, some of the most interesting as well as the most painful months in my life. In 1920 there were ninety-two churches in Toronto and ninety-five picture theatres. Our business was with the latter; our job to persuade the managers of those theatres to exhibit our films in preference to those of Metro-Goldwyn, Warners and Fox. The business was highly competitive, and it was conducted entirely in Yiddish, the managers of the theatres and the salesmen who sold the films being Jews.

I was attached for the purpose of learning the ropes to Jake Berman, the senior salesman, a fat, jolly Jew with pendulous cheeks and rotund paunch, who had sold films all his life and knew the business backwards. We had our stars, now long set but in those days objects of profound passion to a public who had no other entertainment except vaudeville. It was their names that we sold, names like Mary Miles Minter and Tom Mix. We carried with us seductive stills, just as a book salesman carries book jackets. We described in lyrical terms the themes of the films. We named gigantic sums which we had put into making them, and said we expected to gross half a million, a million, a million and a half. Our job was to get bookings and we left no wile untried, no lie untold, no fact unexaggerated, which would enable us to achieve that object. We dealt with strange men who appeared unable or unwilling to speak English. I stood by in Christian simplicity and ignorance while Jake waged his mighty battles and those reluctant purchasers were won over. At least Jake told me afterwards that that was what was happening, for I could not understand a word that they said.

After a month Jake said, 'Ready to try it on your own, kiddo?' and I was given some small suburban theatres of Toronto to cut my teeth on. I lacked Jake's fire as well as his knowledge, but I got some results. Heavy-eyed men chewed cigars and looked at me broodingly while in a low and urgent voice I described the films I had to sell and begged their interest. Men are very kind, even villainous-looking ones, and some of them gave me orders which I took back to the office with pride. But I was not a great success, and I think it must have been with a feeling of relief that the manager found a job for me where I would be out of the way, and would not trouble him and his salesmen with my elementary blunderings in a highly-charged pursuit.

The Canadian Government had made a full-length feature film to demonstrate the dangers of venereal disease, and had arranged with Paramount to distribute it. This horrific, and at the same time appallingly sentimental, document was called 'Open Your Eyes', and it had been booked in theatres throughout the Province on a basis that involved no risk for the exhibitor. He was to have fifty per cent of the takings. My job was to accompany this film to each theatre, to make sure that nobody under sixteen got in to see it, check the takings at the end of each performance, pay over his share to the exhibitor, and send the balance back to our office in Toronto.

For three months until Christmas-time I was engaged on this unenlightening work. The week before Christmas was the last booking, and two days before the holiday I returned to Toronto, glad to be free of a distasteful job, and positively looking forward to the New Year and to taking up my work of selling films again. I felt I had reached a low ebb in my struggle to get on in the world, but I had not quite reached the depths. In my pay envelope was an extra week's wages, and a typed notice to say that my services would not be required after December 31st. I had $50 in hand; I had failed again. It was midwinter, and I was out of work.

CHAPTER NINE

IN the summer, soon after I had come to Toronto, the Temiskaming mine had closed down, and my father had gone to Brule, in the Rocky Mountains between Edmonton and Vancouver, to take over for Bickell and his associates the management of the Blue Diamond coal mine. The deal for the Dolly Varden property had fallen through, and this was another venture to which they had turned. The Blue Diamond, which produced over 2000 tons of coal a day, supplied the Canadian National Railway with all the coal it used between there and the coast. It had sounded to me very far away from Toronto. It seemed further as I lay on my bed, and contemplated the icicles on the window and my own bleak future, and tried to find an explanation for it all.

When I could see no solution, I wondered what I would do next. I thought I might be in for a long siege, so I decided to husband my resources, to buy a pint of milk and two rolls for breakfast, a pint of milk and a sandwich for lunch, and to go to a cafeteria for soup and pie and coffee at night. At this rate I thought that I could last a couple of weeks while I tried to find another job.

I put up with about three or four days of this harsh existence until I found myself both ravenously hungry and appallingly depressed. I began to feel very sorry

for myself, and after lying on my bed all one afternoon,
watching the icicles on the window-sill and the dun-
coloured sky, I walked out that evening to a Canadian
Pacific telegraph office and wired my father that my
job had finished, I was broke, and could he wire me
the money to come home.

It was a terrible defeat for me for several reasons.
My father did not like failure in his own family; he
particularly would not like it, that was certain, if it
involved him with a friend and colleague. He was
certain to be very angry on that score. Then as to
money, it would cost at least $75 to go from Toronto
to Brule. My telegram had asked for the fare, but
would he remember to allow enough for a berth and
for meals? My hunger cried out in me with anxiety.
Finally, this meant the end of my independence. For
three years, since the early months of 1918, except for
that interval in Cobalt, I had been on my own, answer-
able to no one, building up in my own mind a picture
of myself as a man of the world, and in the minds of
others, I hoped, particularly my father whom I was
most anxious to impress, an impression of myself as a
gifted, industrious young man, making his way in the
world, moving steadily and purposefully up the bottom
rungs of the ladder.

Nobody had known until now of the hideous dis-
crepancies between this picture and the real facts: between the successful young man portrayed in my letters
home, and the idle young one, with a dreaming mind
not always dreaming of pure things; the young man
with no money, but with a whole range of sensual
tastes gasping for gratification. I had longed for life.
The bootleg saloons, where I had drunk cheap beer

which I couldn't afford, not for intoxication, but to feel myself a man: the cheap joints, the poker games, the raffish hotels where I had joined in illicit drinking: all this, not for the individual pleasures afforded, which were doubtful and fleeting, but for the sense they gave me that I was being gathered up warmly to the breast of life.

Then there was agony until my father replied, which it took him several days to do. I think perhaps that he supposed I had exaggerated my penury; I believe he thought by his hesitation to reprove me for asking for money.

But finally the cheque came. It was for the exact amount of the fare, nothing more. It came accompanied by a letter which somewhat stiffly welcomed me home, hoped I had got into no trouble, concluded I now meant to settle down. Good God, that was my one desire. Did he not guess how passionately I longed for that?

I bought my ticket, and started off in the train at evening time from Toronto, prepared to sit up in the day coach for the three days' journey to Edmonton. I was going west, away from the comparatively close area of Toronto, Ottawa, Montreal, in which I had had my troubled being ever since I had arrived in Canada three years before.

The first night passed restlessly while the train shuddered northward through the night landscape. When dawn broke we were in Northern Ontario, skirting slowly an immense frozen lake. Outcroppings of rock in the snow-covered ground, and fir trees, their branches laden with a recent fall of snow, were the only features of the view other than this great body of tumbled ice. The heat of the coach had misted the windows, and I saw this only after wiping the screen away. The impression I got was of an immense, brooding solitude; framed in the watery expanse made by my elbow on the window, I saw for the first time the primitive land locked in the iron clamp of winter.

The train crawled across the frozen landscape. Hour succeeded tedious hour throughout the day, while the wastes of snow moved in majestic procession past the train's windows. Little settlements emerged occasionally into view. For hours there would be nothing but the procession of telegraph poles, then suddenly there would spring from the ground a water-tank, a huddle of frame buildings, and a station. The train would jerk to a stop, its bell ringing steadily. Men in mackinaws with caps over their ears would hang about some task in connection with the train, and we would emerge from the steam-heated coaches into the frozen, lifeless air. The first breath was painful to take; it caught at the windpipe, it pinched the nostrils together, the eyeballs shuddered with the sudden shock and watered painfully. Then, stamping our feet, we would make our way to the lunch counter and eat apple-pie and drink coffee, looking with wonder at these people who lived their whole life in this appalling isolation. What would happen when the train pulled away, and they were abandoned in this immensity of snow?

Another day after Winnipeg, and another night. Hour after hour the train drew its length across this white unmarked world. Occasionally a bigger town would appear, and there would be much shunting, much clanging of the train bell as we picked a respectful way across its limits.

My father welcomed me stiffly, and this confirmed the feeling I had that I had now reached the lowest point in the graph of my life. I was a failure. I accepted myself as such, and I think my father did too. I had tried everything, and had stuck to nothing, and after three years had come home, unable to find work anywhere else. I could only be an unskilled labourer, paid the lowest rate, working underground in a coal mine, fetching and carrying for the black-visaged miners who were mostly of foreign origin, chiefly Poles and Ukranians. No mention was made of my heart trouble.

I ceased to try to write; I ceased even to read books. In Brule I frequented the Pool Room instead of the beer parlour, and spent much of my spare time playing poker. I lost the faith I had always had that the future would be better than the present. I saw ahead of me only years of dreary uncongenial work, and I tried to forget this melancholy prospect by becoming hard and tough in my attitude to the world.

Then suddenly a piece of luck came my way. Two thousand five hundred men were employed at the Blue Diamond mine. The reserves of coal in the mountain-side were enormous. The only threat to the contract Bickell had with the Government-owned railway came from the United Mine Workers of America, who were beginning to extend their Union activities into the Province. Union leaders had already been to other mines to address the men. I heard my father and Bickell talking often and anxiously about this, and one night after dinner an idea struck me with blinding force.

Brule was two hundred miles from Edmonton and eight hundred from Vancouver. Between the two metropolises there was a waste of spectacular scenery, the heaving range of rocky snow-capped mountains cupping green valleys below, then the Fraser valley leading to Vancouver and the Pacific coast. Brule was situated near the head of the Yellowstone Pass, a narrow defile through which the old fur traders had made their way, and through which the railway now crept. Brule was hemmed in by these great mountains, its only link with the outside world this narrow track of steel. The miners were earning high wages, but they had nothing to spend them on except beer and gambling. Some families saved their money and took spring trips to the coast. Others, less capable of such sustained saving, took occasional journeys to Edmonton. But most of them stayed in Brule, and this little community of ten thousand souls, shut off from the world in a Shangri-La of isolation, had nothing to do but brood upon mischief, make love to each other's wives, gamble and drink to excess, get into fights and into trouble in every possible way. With so much spare time on their hands, looking always for some new excitement or trouble, they were ideal subjects for conversion to unionism.

The only amenity offered by the mine was a Social Hall in which on Saturday nights there were dances, the music provided by an amateur orchestra recruited from the miners, and once a week a free film show put on by the management. One mounted police corporal supervised the maintenance of the law; the hoosegow in which prisoners were detained was built into his house. Saturday night was his busiest time, and until dawn broke on Sunday morning, the drunken songs and the quarrelsome shouts of boisterous revellers, or those who were protesting their innocence, would emanate from the iron-barred cell at the side of his house. The magistrates' court sat in Jasper each Monday, and on that morning of each week, winter and summer, the Corporal would set off by speeder along the transcontinental tracks with his prisoners handcuffed and looking dejected, and with another citizen of the town commandeered to act as guard. I went often on such trips, which were very enjoyable from a scenic point of view. On a conveyance like a small flat box-car, motored by a gas-engine, we would sweep along the railway line between the high mountains, sometimes having to jump off when we heard a train coming from the opposite direction and lift the speeder off the rails and stand and wait while a mile-long freight drew its slow length by.

I put it to Bickell and my father that unless we offered some alternative interest the U.M.W.A. would make a convert of every man in the place.

Then, on the spur of the moment, I unfolded my proposal for an alternative interest. I said if Bickell would give me an office and lend me a few hundred dollars, I would start a weekly newspaper devoted to local affairs; that I would get people's interest in that way, and when I had that interest I could subtly offset the U.M.W.A. propaganda. As I talked, stimulated by the growing seriousness with which Bickell and my father listened to me, I developed the plan which suddenly became as clear as crystal to me, and which I saw as certain to succeed. And suddenly I knew, too, that I was on sure ground. At last, almost by accident, I had found a means of doing the one thing in the world that I most ardently wanted to do.

Before the evening was over, Bickell had promised

me a rent-free office, and had guaranteed to back my
printing bills up to $300. I would get no pay, but I
could regard the paper as my own, and keep any profit
I made from it.

The next morning I did not report with my shift to
go down the mine. Instead, bathed and breakfasted,
I walked down to the office with my father at nine
o'clock, and he took me to the little separate office,
which stood beside the general store, and was used
occasionally by the auditors on their visits, which from
this moment on was to be the office of the *Blue Diamond
Weekly*. I was to be my own editor, reporter, and
advertisement and circulation manager; all I was given
was a desk, a typewriter and a room. I brought down
from the house after lunch an Oxford Dictionary and
an Atlas, the former because it lent a literary air to the
room, the latter to guide me in the leading articles I
had dreamt all night of writing on the affairs of the
world.

But first I had to find a printer, and to this problem,
when I had been asked about it last night, I had had
a ready answer. I would have the paper printed in
Edmonton, sending in the copy each night by train,
going in each Wednesday to put it together, and waiting
at Brule station each Saturday morning to collect the
printed copies. I could not see why it should not work,
but on the first morning I knew that before anything
else I must needs catch my printer.

I had not the slightest idea how to go about this,
but I took the train to Edmonton that night, and over
breakfast at the Shasta Café pondered the problem.
Then I borrowed the telephone directory from the
young lady at the cash desk. At the back of it I found

a classified directory, and under 'Printers' a list of half a dozen names. None of them meant anything to me, and I do not know why I picked out the particular firm I did, perhaps because it was nearest to the Shasta Café. I went there right away, and asked the girl operating the telephone at a reception desk if I could see the manager.

'What is it in connection with ?' she enquired coldly, suspecting, I think, that I was looking for a job.

'In connection with printing a newspaper,' I replied grandly.

'Oh,' she said, looking at me with surprise.

She slipped off her stool and disappeared behind a swing door. A few minutes later she reappeared and asked me to follow her. I went along a narrow passage lined with glassed-in offices, and was shown into a room where a man of thirty or so sat at a desk in his shirt-sleeves. Through the glass windows I could see the printing shop. In this room I could feel the throb of the presses, so like the throb of the mill stamps that had been the constant audible accompaniment to my young and happy years. I felt a thrill of happiness and excitement. I had never before in my life known this surge of excitement and certainty. This was to be my printer; here was my working partner in the tremendous enterprise to which I had put my hand.

I was not dismayed that he came on grudgingly. I told him the whole story of what I was proposing, of the backing that I had, of the paper I dreamed of building. He raised all the practical difficulties, and I brushed them aside. He said I would be bound to lose money and I said that I wouldn't. He said that small-town papers always failed, and I said that this one was

not going to. Under the pressure of his opposition I
developed new ideas to win subscribers and advertising
income, ideas which I had not thought of until that
moment. Finally he said, 'O.K. then, we will try it.
But we have got to have our bills paid, and if you can't
meet them, then, brother, it's farewell.'

After he had shown me over the shop, and I had
thrilled to touch and to be near these great dark
machines the way my father, I suppose, thrilled to be
near a mill stamp, we were good friends, and he suggested that we should go off and have lunch together.
By this time we had warmed to first-name terms, and
Pete was offering me advice on what he thought would
be circulation-getting features of the paper. I had revealed the utter lack of knowledge I had of type faces
and sizes, of advertisement mats, and the whole secret
science of putting print on pages, and Pete in paternal
fashion was saying, 'I'll see you through that one. You
concentrate on supplying the copy.'

This was the first thing I had ever built myself which
I was committed to show to the world. There was the
same creative excitement I had known before with
everything I had ever written, but there was not the
same after-effect of literary composition, when the
coming together of idea and execution had to survive
scrutiny. There was no time for scrutiny here. Four
pages had to be filled, news of the outside world
summarized, leaders written, local events reported,
entertainments invented, advertisements collected, and
the whole typed out by my inexperienced fingers. It
took fifteen to eighteen hours a day. I quickly found
that I could not do without assistance. There were two
school teachers in Brule; the younger, Earl Samis,

who had one arm, and who refereed all the local football and ice-hockey games, jumped at the idea of becoming sports editor, unpaid. He had a bright and amusing style, and soon wrote the whole of the back page. Mrs. Light, renowned for her cooking, contributed some recipes, added some hints to housewives, and soon with the assistance of some of her friends was occupying half of page three. The rest by superhuman effort I wrote myself, and driven by the necessity of keeping to a time-table, was forced to forgo the purple additions which had disfigured my style, to its great advantage and greater readability.

It was a small-town paper. Few people had a radio then, and television had not been invented. I had no distractions to compete with for the attention of the town. I noticed that the more I indulged in personalities and local gossip the better the circulation. I began by printing 1500 copies. As the weeks passed I increased the printing number to 1800, then to 2500, at which figure, at 10 cents a copy, and with an advertisement revenue of $150 an issue, I was beginning to make money.

I ventured as far as Jasper to collect subscribers and advertisements. Jasper Park Lodge had not then been built, but the small and pretty town was the headquarters of the Park, and becoming well known for the tours Fred Brewster, the famous guide, was arranging through the mountains. Jasper did not have a paper. I commissioned somebody to act as local correspondent, and tried to make the paper serve both towns. The *Blue Diamond Weekly* was thriving, and so was I. For the first time in my life I had money in the bank.

The only cloud on the horizon was the prospect of

a strike. Miners out of work would not be reliable
subscribers, and advertisers would not feel like spending
money at such a time. Besides, my rent-free office was
a payment in kind from the Company for whatever
modest effort I could make to influence the men against
a strike. The trouble is that if you are a writer you have
to write the truth as you see it. I had honestly meant to
defend the Company's point of view, but I found I had
a new responsibility, and one that I could not possibly
avoid : that was, the point of view of my subscribers.

The view the Company took was that unions were
evil in themselves ; they were conspiracies to defraud
the owners. That was all right : that was a viewpoint
which they were entitled, and even expected, to hold.
But they went a step further. They said that the whole
of the town was Company property, and any Union
official setting foot in it would be regarded as a tres-
passer, and Corporal Birks, the Mountie, had instructions to turn him off. This view I could not defend,
and unable to defend it, or in the interests of my
readers to ignore it, I had to attack it. My father was
amused at my presumption, but Jack Bickell wasn't.
He 'phoned my father from Toronto and told him so.

We were advised that the U.M.W.A. was going to
put this theory to the test. A well-known official of
the Union named Ryan announced that he would be in
Brule on a certain date, and would address a meeting of
the men at the Mine Hotel, which was really an enormous dormitory where the single men lived, but which
reserved a few rooms for guests.

On the appointed day Ryan arrived. He had come
on the overnight train from Edmonton, the Transcontinental, so he arrived early in the morning at the

station which was three miles away from the mine. A branch line ran down the side of the hill to the station, taking down full freight cars of coal and bringing back empties two or three times a day. We were all accustomed to ride in the brake-car with the train conductor. But this branch line was undoubtedly Company property, and the conductor had been instructed to refuse to take Ryan aboard. With some local sympathizers, he had to walk up the three miles of tracks, an experience which he didn't enjoy, and said so to me, I having introduced myself as the editor of the local paper, and having been identified by his supporters as the boss's son. He looked at me in a very hostile way, but I said I was footslogging it with him not on my father's behalf, but to report the matter to my readers, and if he didn't want me to accompany him, all right, but that fact would go into the record.

Although this man was a threat to my livelihood, and though he and my father were opposed on an issue which both of them regarded as fundamental, I could not help rather liking him. He was a large, raw-boned Irishman who could not have been in Canada for many years, for he still had traces of the brogue. He looked as though he could use his fists. I thought of my slender father and hoped they wouldn't clash.

This, as it turned out, was just what happened. The meeting had been called for six o'clock, and half an hour before that time nearly a thousand men had collected on the side of the hill outside the front of the hotel. I was on the verandah of the hotel, and was busy composing in my mind sentences which would figure in my description of this vivid scene.

Just after six o'clock, Ryan came out of the front

door of the hotel, accompanied by half a dozen of the miners. The men cheered. He smiled and waved at them, then in the most natural way possible, and very persuasively, began to speak about the brotherhood of working men, and what they could do for one another all over the world if only they would stand together.

At this point in Ryan's oration I saw my father pushing his way through the crowd, followed by Corporal Birks, splendid in his crimson tunic. My father jumped the few feet up onto the platform and walked up to Ryan. He had his back to the crowd. He looked very slight in front of Ryan.

'Now, my friend,' he said in a loud voice. 'This is Company property, and you are trespassing. You are disturbing the peace. I'll give you five minutes to get off this platform and out of town.' He looked at his wrist-watch expressively, and then stood with one hand in the pocket of his jacket, the other holding a riding-crop which he slapped against his polished riding-boots.

Ryan waited for the crowd to get their voice in, and they lost no time. 'Let him speak. He's doing no harm. We've got a right to hear what he has to say.' This emerged from a general hubbub, together with a good deal of lurid profanity, cat-calls and whistles.

I heard my father cry, 'A minute left, Ryan!' but Ryan folded his broad arms across his chest and struck an attitude which certainly showed no intention of moving. I had a momentary flash of admiration for him before my father, looking at his watch, slapped his boot extra hard, then grabbed Ryan by the elbows and turned him towards the edge of the verandah. At which the giant suddenly awoke. The look of an Irishman succumbing to the intoxication of a fight swept across his face. His folded arms parted, his huge hands enclosed my father's waist, and he lifted him like a sack and threw him off the platform.

In a moment there was a great commotion, and the editor of the *Blue Diamond Weekly* forgot his mission to report all this objectively. With a yell I jumped at Ryan's back and put my arm round his neck. I could hear him grunt with the shock. Then I felt myself plucked from behind by the shirt-collar and pulled to the ground, and I saw Corporal Birks move in and take command. The red tunic, the look in his eyes, his parade-ground voice and the revolver he took from his holster had us all in a moment posed as in a *tableau vivant*. Even the thousand men grouped below us were suddenly silent.

'I am going to book you for assault,' said Corporal Birks to Ryan.

'That's right, Corporal,' said my father, picking himself up. 'Put him in the clink for tonight. I am going to make a charge for trespassing and assault.'

The case was heard before the magistrates in Jasper the following week. I wrote a full account of it for the *Blue Diamond Weekly* and for the *Edmonton Journal*, who had begun to accept and pay me for items of local interest that I sent in to them. Ryan was fined $50 for assault, and the magistrates ruled that the Company had the right to forbid anyone access to the property.

I wrote a long editorial on the subject, trying to be as fair as I could to both sides, but I concluded by saying that legal restraints and injunctions had never prevented men from uniting if they strongly desired to do it, and I suggested that the owners would be well advised to meet the men by admitting the Union, rather than wait for the inevitable to happen. I realized that I was signing my own discharge in writing this. I told my father so, but said I could not write anything else.

He said, 'I wish you did not feel you have to, son. But if that is what you think, I would rather you said so than that you said what you think would please us, because we're the side your bread is buttered on.

'But,' he added, 'I don't see how you can keep the paper going in these circumstances.'

'I know. I've thought of that. But I don't see what else I can do. It means going back to the pit, or going away and trying to find a job. I'd like to try something else, Dad. I'd like to go to a university. Do you think I could?'

What I meant was, would he support me for three years, but I was too shy to say so, and as usual, it didn't seem to occur to him. It had been the same when I said I was going into the R.A.F. He had thought it was a spunky thing to do. Now that I wanted to get on in the world, he said he thought that would be fine. He did not say, as other people's fathers would surely have done: 'Good for you, old son. I'll back you up. You will need money. Don't worry about that. Go ahead, I'm proud of you.'

I wrote to the University of Alberta, and asked what qualifications I would need. They answered that I would need to have matriculated. I went to see the senior schoolmaster at Brule and asked him what matriculation was. He was a fine old man, called Mr. Austen, white-haired, plump, worn and benevolent, a born pedagogue whose delight it was to teach. He questioned me thoroughly about what stage I had reached at Berkhamsted, and when I could not give very clear answers, he wrote himself to the school for my record. This showed that I had not reached the stage of matriculation, and as I had been out of school for six years, I was a good deal below the standard required by the university. Mr. Austen now warmed to his task, and offered to coach me.

The formidability of the gap I had to make up frightened me, and if he had been less urgent my resolution might have failed. I agreed to go to school four nights a week, after my working day was done. We settled a fee for this which I knew I would have to pay out of my wages, and the long haul began. I had five subjects to cover. The nights were cold, and I was weary after a day working in the mine. But they were just as cold for Mr. Austen: it must have been even more uninviting for him to face an evening in the schoolroom after a long day spent there with the miners' children.

At first we worked stiffly; my mind was, as it were, muscle-bound; he must have had some provoking hours battering against the walls of my ignorance; I had some tedious ones waiting for the light of understanding to break in. Slowly it came, just a glimmer at first, then a dull glow. Mr. Austen fanned it frenziedly, and I ached with the effort to comprehend, and then to contain what it appeared I had comprehended. We were both beside ourselves with exhaustion when I finally sat for the examination in the schoolroom at Jasper. He met me at the station on my return. I could not tell him how I had done. All right, I guessed.

No, not all right, I thought. Oh, I don't know. How can I tell? I was irritated with the old man for pressing me, and for clinging to my arm as we walked up the hill to the town, comforting me, probing me with his questions, cheering me up, swallowing his exaggerated hopes. I was glad to shake him off, and I avoided him for the next few weeks until the word came that I had passed. I bought a bottle of whisky from the local bootlegger, and went to his house to celebrate. We made a night of it together, that white-haired old school-master and I, twenty-one, and starting the long upward climb.

In the last days of September I went to Edmonton and registered at the university as a Freshman. My father said that he would pay my fees, board and room for the first year, but that I must take a job in the summer and earn enough myself to pay the second year. He was earning at this time twenty thousand dollars a year, but it was not meanness on his part to insist that after the first year I should keep myself. This was Canadian practice. 'Working your way through' was what everybody did, even if there was no need for it. The long vacation from the beginning of May until the beginning of October provided for that, and I should have been ashamed; it would have looked as though I were delicate or queer, not to have followed the universal custom. And to tell the truth, I did not look that far ahead. Next summer was for me as the next life is for many people, something to be faced one day, but at an infinite remove in time.

CHAPTER TEN

THERE was something symbolic to me in the very
site where the university stood, high on the bluffs
above the swift-flowing North Saskatchewan
River. It bore to the untidy straggling town below the
eminence and remoteness that the Acropolis bears to
Athens. I had no aesthete's eye. My life had been spent
in mining camps where the coal-tip and the slag-
heap or the ugly-shaped chimneys of the refinery or the
mill-house were the prominent features of the landscape.
I was no judge of beauty, but these plain rectangular
brick buildings with windows cased in stone, fronting
onto a green quad which was criss-crossed by board
walks, to save the tender grass in the summer, to sur-
mount the snow in the winter; all this seemed to me
impressive. There was not a tree in sight. Though no
ancient chapel or Gothic archway, no cloister where one
might walk in contemplation, marked this academic
scene, as they had some of those which I had read about
in books, yet I was thrilled by it. A brightness seemed
to me to fall from the air. The season was at its sweetest;
the sun shone mellowly, the air was invigorating; I
felt myself drawn irresistibly into a large company of
the élite, and experienced such a surge of happiness as I
had not known for many years.

This lasted but a day or two until the Sophomores
descended upon me and upon all Freshmen. There was

a two-week period of initiation. Our heads were
shaved; we were made to wear foolish skull-caps
quartered in the university colours, green and gold.
Some people, with an equanimous disposition, cheerful,
contented with life, can put up with the small indignities
and unworthinesses it occasionally inflicts, but others,
lean and tense, and as nervous as horses, cannot. I was
one of the latter kind. I hated every moment of those
two weeks. I hated the practical jokes, being tipped
out of bed in the dead of night, and made to walk
blindfold along a plank, not knowing how high it was
above the floor, being commanded to jump, and flinging
myself wildly with knees bent and falling heavily onto
a hardwood floor perhaps only eighteen inches below.
I hated having a razor, heated in a candle flame, passed
over my vital part, after an earnest discussion had taken
place as to whether it should be amputated, and the
decision had been in favour of the operation. I hated
as much being held down and blindfolded while these
tortures were practised. I hated the laughter which was
the constant accompaniment to them, and by the end
of the period I had worked up such a state of contemptuous anger towards this band of brothers whom I
had thought to be the élite that I was ready there and
then to leave the university, and was stopped only by
images in my mind of the stricken face of Mr. Austen,
of my father's wounded gaze, shamed by my incapacity
to stand up to my fellow-men, disappointed once more
by my inability to stick to anything.

The initiation period was followed by a night of
reconciliation when the Sophomores entertained the
Freshmen to a theatre, and we snake-danced up and
down Jasper Avenue. I joined in the merriment, but

my heart felt bruised, and for a few weeks I kept moodily to myself while I made an effort to use my brain again, after so long having worked with my hands. I did not find it easy, and when the snow came I was thoroughly out of sorts and unhappy.

At twenty-one I was about three years older than the other Freshmen; I was about the age of a Senior, but as far beneath them as a snake's belly is below an elephant's ear. But there were a dozen or so students even older. These were men who had returned from the war in 1919 and had begun the long medical course which took six years. They kept together, eating at one table in Athabasca Hall, and meeting in each other's rooms. The presiding spirit of this little group was a small man of delicate features and large luminous grey eyes named Mark Levy. He noticed my moodiness, having the sharp eyes of a good doctor in the making, and invited me to join their table. This I did, and found myself immediately much happier, until in the following week the University Magazine carried a note of advice in its column of comment on affairs, reminding Mark Levy that you can't make a silk purse out of a sow's ear, and suggesting that 'a certain Freshman' should not be spoiled by too much attention.

I wanted to leave the table, but Mark told me to ignore this. The others acted like a bodyguard and closed in round me with their friendship, and when I went home at Christmas I was feeling much better. Except about my work. We had a series of tests, and I more than suspected that I had not distinguished myself except in my favourite subject, English.

When I returned in January, my suspicions were confirmed. I was invited to see the Dean; he asked me some searching questions, but the search did not reveal the reason for my failure. I thought I was working, but I had not yet learnt that work without concentration is mere dumb-show.

I had by this time got to the point where I anticipated failure from everything I tried, and I had fallen into the bad habit of bluffing my way along as far as possible. In this matter Nature was helping me. I had been a round-faced, clear-eyed, very healthy and innocent-looking boy. The hard physical work I had now done since I was sixteen had thinned me down considerably, and at the same time I had shot up in height so that I was now six feet one and a half inches tall and weighed only 150 pounds, and was an object of tender concern to any lady with a maternal instinct. Older men also generally took a sympathetic view of me, I suppose because I had come to have a sort of gravity of counten-ance that looked reliable and deserving of encourage-ment, but they were more quickly disillusioned than the ladies. The Dean and I had a series of interviews that ended with his losing his patience, and reminding me that I must pass at the end of the year or not return next Fall. Pass in the end I did. I was to be allowed to go on; I had now only to find the means.

That summer gave me a wonderful opportunity to recruit my health, diminished by my first winter spent indoors since 1919. The Canadian National Railways were opening a new hotel at Jasper in the Rocky Mountains. Eight chauffeurs were needed to drive tourists to the scenic beauty spots accessible by motor road. The intention was to use undergraduates, and to select them from the various Western universities. I applied with others, and had the luck to be chosen, with another young man, Aubrey Macmillan, from the Alberta contingent.

We spent long days in the open air from three to six thousand feet above sea-level, driving our rich clients to Maligne Canyon or Mount Edith Cavell and to Fort Henry, which was the limit of the motor roads in those days. We chauffeurs slept together in a dormitory above the garage where our cars were kept, and ate together in a Mess Hall. It was a wonderful long summer from May until the beginning of October. We were paid $75 a month, and given a uniform and full keep. The tourists were generous with tips, which we all learned after a preliminary phase of embarrassment, not only to accept, but to feel defrauded of if, out of excessive delicacy, they were not offered. I learned to gauge my passengers with an eye to their potential contributions, and to waste little time on those who shook hands heartily at the end, without leaving anything in one's hand, and to devote my attention to those who at the end of a day trip would say, 'I guess you could use this, feller,' and pass a five- or ten-dollar bill across.

Once, the President of the Bank of Montreal signed a fifty-dollar bill, which had his likeness engraved on it, and gave it to me, saying, 'You collect autographs?' Once a rich and lovable old New Yorker, whom I had driven about for several days without drawing from him any response or recompense, said to me, 'Would you like to come and spend Christmas with us, son? I got two daughters. Never had a boy. Be glad if you would come.' Late that autumn he wrote me to the university to reinforce the invitation, offering to send me a return ticket if I would come. With such high adventures the summer passed, and when the hotel closed and it was time to return to the university I had nearly one thousand dollars saved, with my pay and my tips.

I was entering upon my Sophomore year, and it fell to me to bully the Freshmen. But I had no heart for such matters, remembering only too well what I had suffered only a year before. Besides, I was suddenly in a hurry to get on with life. Having passed my exams, I was entering upon a much more interesting university year. I had grounds for thinking that some merit in me would at last be recognized. I knew by the standards that prevailed that I could write far better and more fluently than most people. The course that proved the stumbling-block for most people in their second year of Arts was English 2, a course entitled 'English Prose from Bacon to Hardy', given by Professor Broadus, the head of the English Department, who was reputed by those not at ease with their language and literature to be a holy terror, and by those who had survived the course with distinction to be the greatest and most inspiring teacher of English in North America.

Broadus was a legendary figure in that small upland world. He had been teaching at Harvard when a tubercular gland in his neck put him in a sanatorium. That was in 1909, just at the time when Dr. Tory, the newly-appointed president of Alberta University, was recruiting his first staff from the universities on the coast. Broadus was told that he must live in the West; Tory was advertising for teachers for his foundling. They met; they took to each other. Harvard, where Broadus had taught, and Radcliffe, where Mrs Broadus had been teaching, were left behind. Edmonton, to the Boston of that time, was almost as remote as the Yukon, and Broadus must indeed have been a dying man, in the eyes of his Cambridge friends, if the demands of his health could drive him to take up a teaching post in a university sprung out of the great plains where but a few years before buffaloes and Indians had roamed, and the Mountie had dispensed law and made order prevail. The banks of the Saskatchewan seemed very far away from Boston Common and the Faculty Club.

English 2, where I first came into contact with this great man, was compulsory for all second-year people proceeding to an Arts Degree, and was a hazardous course designed wickedly by Broadus to trap the worthy into specialization in English, and to undermine, destroy and overwhelm those who took the subject lightly.

He quickly pounced on my pretensions. When our first themes were returned with his markings, I saw to my absolute amazement that I had failed. I thought there must have been some mistake. I folded back the foolscap pages, certain that I would find that there had been an error; he must have mixed my work with that of someone else.

But there was no mistake. Shame, oh, burning shame! Some of my finest phrases were heavily underscored; the sentiments they expressed ridiculed in the margins. The construction of some of my sentences was shown to be faulty, and the verbosity and fulsomeness of my style laid bare with a prick of his waspish pen. I could have wept with embarrassment and injured pride. This was the best I could do, and he could only scoff at it. I began to hate him, and I longed to get even with him, and I ended up by going to his room in the Arts Building that afternoon to argue it out with him.

He was a little man with a large and rather fine head which perpetually shook and trembled like a flower on a long stalk. He wore gold-rimmed spectacles from behind which his eyes looked coldly. He smoked without ceasing, when one cigarette was nearly done stubbing it out with his brown wooden holder, and replacing it with a new one.

He wasted little time with me over the preliminaries.

'I don't know who you are,' he said. 'You've told me your name, but it means nothing to me, and will continue to mean nothing until you can distinguish yourself in some way. Your essay was one of the worst in the whole class. I can understand the son of an immigrant Lithuanian farmer finding difficulty with the English language, but you are Canadian or British and this is your native tongue, and you've abused it more in these few pages than any of these ignorant youths who have been speaking it for a few years.

'Who in God's name told you that you can write? I can see that somebody has flattered you in that way. Well, let me tell you plainly that you can't, and you will fail this course unless you recognize that fact and cease to show off about something for which you haven't the slightest skill.

'I don't want any excuses or explanations. If I have to mark that revolting, nauseatingly pompous essay of yours again, I will mark it even harder. Go away. Depart. Avaunt. Get out of my sight, man, until you can hold your head up and look me in the eye, and say "I have really tried". Goodbye.'

P

The next I knew, I was out in the hall, my cheeks burning, my mind blazing, not with anger but with a strange kind of excitement. I was determined to show this old man that I was no ordinary undergraduate. After all, I had edited a paper. I had since then con- tributed a full-page article to the *Edmonton Journal* in commemoration of the shooting of Edith Cavell. He might not think much of my style, but I could earn a living with it. It might not do for English 2, but it did for the *Edmonton Journal*. I would show him.

Ever busy with my pen — my poor pen, held now in such scorn — I had been amusing myself during the summer at Jasper with writing parodies of well-known poems. The fun this exercise offered me was in the contrast it provided between the mellowness of the original and the harsh reality of the matter if a local sub- ject were substituted. I had collected a number of these, and I now interspersed them with some comments after the style of ' Charivaria ' in *Punch*, and had sent them off to Mr. Morrison, the editor of the *Emdonton Journal*. He had used them, setting them out in a column on the editorial page where they looked quite neat and important. He asked me for more, and I warmed to my task. Soon I was providing the *Edmonton Journal* with two and sometimes three full columns a week under the heading 'Hodge-Podge'. I got a good deal of fun out of it and quite a lot of money, but Professor Broadus did not seem to notice that he had a real live author in his English 2 class.

What Broadus did notice was that in the essays I was writing for him, I had ceased to show off. The shock treatment had done me good. My style was now so bare it was nearly indecent, and to hide its nakedness I had to cover it with some facts. Broadus called me to his room, and gave me back an essay bearing rather a high mark. The stony quality of his eyes moistened and softened just for the briefest moment before his head shook everything back into firmness again. 'Come to tea,' he said. 'Come and meet my wife. Call for me at 4.15 this afternoon.'

Not, 'I hope you are free', or 'Would you like to come?' Just a command to be there, and I shivered with satisfaction.

It was November, and the first snow had fallen. It lay like icing on a cake, very white where nothing had touched it, yellow and mud-stained where it had fallen into the ruts of car or sleigh tracks. I accompanied the Professor from his office to the car park. In 1924, cars were still comparatively rare around the university. The Professor's was a Star, 1919 model. Its bonnet was swathed in blankets. Raised high on its little tyres, which were festooned with chains, it looked very leggy and rather plucky. The Professor removed the blankets and stuffed them inside, and then adjusted the spark and the gas levers on the steering-wheel, rubbed his hands together briskly, looked at the starting-handle and looked at me. 'Let me do it,' I said, and he made no difficulty, motioning me with his hand to wait while he adjusted himself in the driver's seat. Then I turned the handle, rocking the little car as I did so, until suddenly it caught fire, gave a tremendous shudder, an ear-splitting single pop from its exhaust, and then reverberated and thundered into roaring life. The Professor beamed at me and opened the door for me to get in beside him, and with a jerk we ran crisply over the snow, heading south along the bank of the river.

'I call him Hotspur,' explained the Professor, and quoted beautifully :

' By heaven, methinks it were an easy leap
To pluck bright honour from the pale-faced moon,
Or drive into the bottom of the deep,
Where fathom-line could never touch the ground,
And pluck up drownéd honour by the locks.'

Hotspur, breasting the snowy road, swam with a swan-like motion along the bank above the river. I marvelled that the Professor could find his way, for out here the snow surface was unmarked by any tracks, and perilously close at our right hand the chasm opened, at the foot of which, sixty or seventy feet below, lay the river, already frozen at its sides. The icy wind whistled through the curtains, but we were happy and relaxed, the day's toil being behind us, and tea and the fireside ahead. I was warmed by a glow of purest friendship for this old man. He had done little except insult me since we had first met, but I somehow knew that afternoon as we swayed, slid and ground our way along the snowy road in gallant Hotspur, that he was going to have a profound and exciting influence on my life. Taking care that he should not observe me, I smiled at him.

The house which Broadus had built was an attractive small one, commanding a lovely view across the river valley. It was totally isolated, even in the summer, and no one ever came to do the rough work. Mrs. Broadus, a lady of exceptional beauty and fine breeding, did all.

She came to greet us as we stamped our way into the lamplit house. I had not met a lady for a very long time ; she stood, as my mother would have stood,

silent and still, and so gracefully, like a figure from a
good painting. Her eyes were like my mother's, not
the same colour, but large and deep and understanding.
Her voice was low like my mother's. I had forgotten.
I was suddenly shy and tongue-tied. My heart raced,
and I trembled. I was so afraid of looking a fool.

Broadus took me up to his study while she went to
the kitchen to get tea. Lamps were lit, and the fire was
burning. I saw bookshelves on four sides of the room
reaching to the ceiling, but still these could not contain
all the books. By his chair was a pile as high as the
arm. By hers there was a footstool, and a piece of
knitting, with the needles still in it, lay where she had
put it down at our coming.

What was it? Where had I been? This book-
lined room, the knitting on the footstool, the hissing
fire, the Professor's voice going on and on. . . . I had
been asleep, I had been having a horrible nightmare.
The terrible things I had done since that day we walked
away from the cemetery, the emptiness, the growing
pain of remorse, the waste, the hopelessness, the despair,
and more than anything, the lack of love, the being
alone: all this was vanishing, and I hardly dared to
speak in case the sound of my voice summoned it all
back again.

I had the grace to rise when Mrs. Broadus came in
bearing a heavy tray, but I was too gauche to take it
from her until the Professor, making ineffectual fumb-
ling to clear the table that stood before the fire, commanded me in tones of thunder to do it. Soon we were
seated round the table, and the spirit-lamp was burning
under the silver kettle, and there on a plate were scones
like those which Keno used to make. And the thinnest

bread and butter. And crab-apple jelly. And an uncut fruit cake. I had not sat down to such a tea since I was a child; for years I had not sat down to tea at all. It was a forgotten pleasure.

I was too self-conscious to make the sort of meal my hungry stomach craved for. The Professor masticated, champed and chawed with great deliberation while Mrs. Broadus sat with a slight smile on her lovely face and drew me out. I had resented Mrs. Elliott's vulgar curiosity, and I had always thought it right to keep my story to myself, but before I knew where I was I was telling this lady all. Well, nearly all. She did not say 'Poor boy,' as Mrs. Elliott had done. She looked at me with amusement and said, 'You have been busy,' and the Professor, finishing his splendid tea at this point, dabbed at his lips with his handkerchief and said, 'Too busy to learn some of the elementary facts of our literature.' He smiled at me to show that this was not offensively meant.

'There are half a dozen young men and women in this class who have an ear for the beauty of language, but there isn't one who has been taught to use it. Is there no home in which books are read any more, just for sheer pleasure?'

He was not asking me the question. He had, even to me, the air of a man indulging himself in a pet irritation.

'Read us something then, dear,' said Mrs. Broadus.

'What shall it be, love?' said the Professor, rising and running his fingers lovingly along the shelves.

'Tonight — Hardy. Don't you agree, Mr. Dickson?'

The Professor withdrew a book and settled himself,

head shaking furiously under the lamplight. There was a moment's silence, and then his voice came, and my heart responded, hammering against my windpipe so that for a moment I could hardly breathe:

'When the Present has latched its postern behind my
    tremulous stay,
And the May month flaps its glad green leaves like
    wings,
Delicate-filmed as new-spun silk, will the neighbours
    say,
"He was a man who used to notice such things" ?'

He read on, and between poems talked about the authors. I leant back in my chair, and shut my eyes against the fire and the light of the room, and listened to this wonderful voice making this beautiful music. It was not until it was over, and I was walking back to the university in the darkness, that I remembered the poetry recitations of my youngest years. What foolish amateurs we had been, what nonsense we had declaimed. It shamed me to think that evening after evening we had sung sentimental songs at the piano, and recited Shelley and Byron. We had never read poetry like this. I had never guessed what music our language could make until I had heard it read aloud that afternoon. It was the sound that gripped me, not the sense of the words. That was to come as I made my way forward with painful slowness from the position I had just won.

CHAPTER ELEVEN

M Y devotion to the Professor became absolute. I worked with passion to earn his praise, and before long found myself doing it because the subject absorbed me. He first awoke in me the ability to concentrate. Until then, I had been like a butterfly, blown by the breeze of my thoughts. Now I learned to shut out from my mind the sights and sounds and distractions of the world as I concentrated on a particular goal. I was driven in this direction at first by the Professor's savage irony. He was like a Regimental Sergeant-Major. The square where we drilled was the whole field of literature. I was the awkward recruit. He drilled me tirelessly until I had reached a point where presumably I would not disgrace the Regiment. Then, like the Sergeant-Major, he started to allow me little pleasures which were presented as privileges. Like the recruit, I did not remember that what were privileges now were really old liberties, once taken for granted.

I had never read any of Jane Austen's books. He read aloud one afternoon the first chapter of *Pride and Prejudice*, and then threw the book at me and said, 'Jane is yours. You lucky ass, to stumble upon such good fortune.' I fell in love with Elizabeth Bennet, and have been faithful to her ever since. But I could not stop with the Bennets. I had to go on and know the Dashwoods, and meet Mrs. Jennings and Mr.

Palmer. I had to read *Mansfield Park*, *Emma*, *Northanger Abbey* and *Persuasion* at a run, and do all my other work too. But once having found Jane, I could not let her go, and the Professor encouraged me to waste my time reading in this way, and pooh-poohed my squeaks of fear about not getting my work done.

It became a habit. He would probe and find out some author whom I had not read, a not very difficult thing to do. Then he would read a sample, and with shaking head and fiendish smile, watch while the potion took. Giddy with rapture, I would succumb. If I made an attempt to break free of the spell at the end of that book, he would scoff at me.

'How can you stand there, having read *The Ordeal of Richard Feverel*, and say that you haven't time to read *The Egoist*. If you liked Richard, how can you stop without knowing Sir Willoughby Patterne, *and* one of the most charming characters in English fiction, the "dainty rogue in porcelain", Clara Middleton? You must really be mad, Rache. You cannot think what you are saying.'

Thus he bullied me and drove me, scoffed at me, humiliated me, and by such unceasing endeavours dragged me like a kicking calf that had been running wild into the paddock of English writing. It was wonderful for me educationally, but it was not psychologically. Though I had to be driven to them at first, books did become a refuge for me, and too often in after life I was inclined to evade facing hard facts by burying my head instead in a book. But my life was there, to be made or to be spoiled, and I think I was lucky that if it had to be imperfect, as most lives have to be, this should have been what marred it. When I look back over the years the Professor, as much as my father, made me what I am.

My father, now very happily remarried, had a fine infant son, and another on the way. He had retired from active mining, and in a characteristic fit of exuberant spendthriftness, as though he had for ever to live, had bought a fruit farm in the Fraser Valley, where, in competition with the Japanese market gardeners, he was putting up a vigorous fight for survival, the object, as long as his small capital lasted, of the attentions of young gentlemen who were salesmen for the agricultural machinery companies. Poor old Dad, he never had a chance in that world. But for the moment he had passed out of my life, and the Professor and Mrs. Broadus became father and mother to me. In the intervals between the university closing and Jasper Park Lodge opening, and again in the Fall when Jasper closed and the university residences had not opened, I stayed at the Little Brown House and thought of it as my home. In term-time I went out only on Sunday afternoons.

In my third and fourth years I read for Honours in English. I wonder now that I did not break down with all I had to do, and the discipline I imposed on myself. I would get up at six in the morning, and go for a run in the snow. Back at six-thirty, I would take a cold shower, have a brisk rub-down, and then work at one of the essays I had to prepare until breakfast at seven forty-five. There were lectures or tutorials for the Honours group for several hours during the day. In the intervals I had to work in the Library. In the evening after dinner I would work at my themes again until eleven-thirty or midnight. Then I would put my books

aside and start to compose my column for the *Journal*.
It would sometimes be as late as two in the morning
before that was done.   Then, when the rest of the
undergraduate world lay asleep, I would put on 'Arctic'
boots, a heavy overcoat and thick muffler, pull my cap
down over the tips of my ears, and go out into the
winter's night to deliver my copy, across the High Level
Bridge, two and a half miles away.

Cold were those nights, but beautiful, and tired
though my body was, it pulsated still with the creative
raptures I had just endured.   Sometimes, when it was
very cold, the Northern Lights would be streaming up
and down the arch of the night sky ; sometimes every
star would be brilliantly cut out in gold against the
steel-blue hood of the heavens.   Below me, as I walked
across the bridge, the river would be silent and white ;
the wind rushing over it would brush up the snow, if it
were newly fallen, and particles of it would sting my
cheeks and nose.   When I left the bridge and walked
through the streets they were empty, but I was no
longer afraid, as I had been only ten years before, when
I walked the night streets of Ottawa on my way to the
Experimental Farm.   I was at home now in this great
wide land.   I was accepted as a Canadian.   I had my
goal in front of me ; I could never be lonely or heart-
broken again.   I was just as short of money, and I was
even more short of sleep than I had been years ago.
But I was no longer afraid.

Except of Mr. Harris.   I was afraid of Alfred Harris.
He had been born, I think, a Baptist minister's son.

Whoever his father and mother were, they had not had the turmoil of matters that had formed the lives of my parents. You only had to look at Alfred Harris to see that. He will, accidents barred, be alive today, and I hope he will forgive me for saying that on his twenty-one-year-old face he wore a look of peace. He had curly hair, pale-blue eyes, a round meditative face, and inside, deep down under this deceptive appearance, a mind that worked like a dynamo.

There were five of us reading for Honours. There were five golden prizes. There was the Lieutenant-Governor's Gold Medal; a prize for the study of Shakespeare, a Chaucer prize. There was a Fellowship in English Literature, given for the highest aggregate marks. There were two other lesser prizes. Like wolves around a camp-fire we circled round these awards, snuffling and moaning and howling in anticipation.

It came to be between Harris and me. In our last year it was plain to us all that he and I were to dispute for these prizes, and the three others stood back to watch, while the Professor, timekeeper of the race, shook violently and whipped us all on with cruel and biting phrases. Alfred Harris bore it all calmly, but now that we were come to the last few months, I could not eat or sleep. I was already pale because of the winter. Now my pallor had a green tinge. Nobody said to me, 'Let up. You are killing yourself.' I was killing myself with work and lack of food and sleep, but nobody interfered. Eleanor Broadus looked at me sorrowfully and sympathetically, but she would no more have told me to stop than one would tell an athlete towards the end of a hard-run race to take it easy, that it did not matter whether he won or not.

When in May the last exam was written, I did not know how I had done. And suddenly, exhausted with the effort, I did not care. I was to go to Jasper on May 15th. Convocation was on that day. But I was so worn out, so sick in body and tired in mind, that I proposed to take my degree *in absentia*. I thought that Harris would have beaten me for the prizes. I almost hoped that he might have done, and thereby have released me from an obligation that I had undertaken, and which now, in my state of mental exhaustion, I regretted.

A month before Finals, during Sunday supper at the Professor's, he had asked me whether I would like to join the teaching staff of the university when I graduated. The lowest grade in the teaching hierarchy was peopled by assistant lecturers. The pay was commensurate with the status of the job, I think $1500 a year. The idea was that the teacher's duties were equally light, and that an assistant lecturer would have time for work on a thesis with the aim of getting an M.A. I had been flattered by the Professor's proposition, the old devil could have flattered me into anything, and it is presumptuous to pretend that I had any decision in the matter. But it was a mark of how I had come on under this man's tutelage — threatened with being thrown out of the university in my Freshman year, and now in my senior year invited to join its staff.

Much had been happening in this last year. I had met a lot of people in Edmonton. This began, I think, because of my column in the *Journal*; I had become in the district a small-scale celebrity, and was invited out that I might be looked at, and might roar like a little lion.   Also I had been at the university now for four years, and was known.   I had fallen secretly in love with a beautiful girl, who was reading for Honours in Mathematics, of all things, a tall stately blonde with wide-spaced grey eyes that melted me when they looked at me.   I never took her out; I was much too shy to ask her.   But she must have felt the weight of my eyes on her, because once she invited me.

The girls' residence was called Pembina, and once a year the seniors at Pembina were allowed under the strict surveillance of the Dean of Women to invite the senior men to a Sunday supper.   As there were three or four men to every woman in the university, it was the pretty custom that each senior girl should invite two men, one to sit on her right hand and one on her left.   It was the custom that the one she particularly favoured should sit on her right hand.

I almost fainted when I received a note from my beautiful blonde, Grace Atkinson, asking me to be her guest at this supper in our senior year.   With what care I bathed and adorned myself for this encounter.   With what trepidation I took myself to Pembina, to be greeted coolly by Grace.   I don't know what I expected. She could not have flung her arms about me and kissed me.   I honestly believed that I had never seen anyone more beautiful.   Her other partner, Eric Stuart, was much more at ease with her.   He joked; he was a man of the world.   Here was I, nearly twenty-five, about to leave the university and go out in the world, in a kind of fashion, and I could not face a girl like this without almost dying.   But, God, she was beautiful, and she made me giddy.

Then two things happened.   I discovered from the

place list that I, not Eric Stuart, was to sit on her right hand. I was her favoured one. Lord, if I only had the sense, I should have accepted the sweet challenge that this implied. But what did I do? I pretended to have noticed nothing unusual. I looked fixedly into a far corner of the room until Miss Dodd, the Dean, came up to me and said, 'Mr. Dickson, I am going to ask you to say Grace tonight.' I giggled, and Miss Dodd looked sharply at me.

I pulled myself together with an effort, realizing that I couldn't share my joke with Miss Dodd by saying 'But Grace has said Rache tonight'. Miss Dodd swept to the head of the table; her stern meaningful look at me conveyed that she hoped I had not been solacing myself with a bottle from the Liquor Commission, and that I would rise to the occasion.

When we were all at our seats, Miss Dodd rose and said, 'Mr. Dickson will say Grace this evening.' We all scrambled to our feet, my hands went wet, my feet cold, my mind went blank. I had listened to the university Grace being said at lunch and dinner every day for four years, and in a calm moment could have recited it word for word. But all I could now remember was the opening phrase, *quaecumque vera*. I remembered our childhood grace, 'For what we are about to receive, O Lord, make us truly thankful', and was about to shrill those words when my maniac eye caught from its corner a glimpse of the corn-coloured hair over the ear of my beloved, standing pensive by my shoulder, her head bent forward. Rightly called Grace. What I could not say in private I could say in public. I knew the standard of Latin in this campus. Only the Honours students in classics, of whom I was

one, would know Catullus. I heard my own voice, as
from a great distance, saying the lovely words I had
learnt only a few weeks before:

> 'Dianae sumus in fide
> Puellae et pueri integri:
> Dianam pueri integri
> Puellaeque canamus.'

A swelling *Amen*, and we all scraped our chairs back
and sat down. Miss Dodd, who was only a few seats
from me, bent forward and said, 'A very nice Grace,
Mr. Dickson. I didn't recognize it.'

'My old school one,' I said unblushingly.

'A change,' said Miss Dodd, 'after *Benedictus
Benedicat*.'

My love was fated never to be told, and that was
a pity. The girl had brains: she was reading for
Honours in mathematics; she was as beautiful as the
Snow Queen. My life might have been utterly different
if I had had the courage to take her hand, as we stood
on the stone steps outside Pembina at 11.30 that night,
and had said 'I love you'.

For the high moment of this special evening had
come. By tradition the left-hand men made their dis-
creet exits, saying goodbye to Miss Dodd, thanking
their particular hostesses. The right-hand man was left
to exact the privilege for which he had been elected to
his position.

The broad front steps of Pembina were clotted with
perhaps twenty couples. Of these Grace and I were

one. I stood a step below her, and she frowned down
at me. It was not the moment to frown, nor was it
the moment to stand as I did, faltering, feeble, like a
eunuch at a saturnalia. My loved one rightly became
vexed.

'You are not really good-looking, you know. You
have a nice face.'

Since this was apropos of nothing that we had said,
for in fact we had said nothing, I swallowed hard and
squeezed her hand.

'Thank you very much, Grace, for asking me.'

I turned away, conscious that I had bungled an
important moment in my life.

Yet I loved her, and thought much about her in
the last few months I spent at the university. But my
mind was already fixed on something else, and that
was, getting on in the world. Driving ambition, the
plant that had grown out of the rough soil of my life
during the last ten years, was ready to wrap itself around
me, to wind me in its coils for ever, and there was no
room for love.

A week before I was to leave for Jasper, and the
evening before the results of our examinations were to
be published, the Professor got me on the 'phone. He
was irritatingly coy and mysterious. He asked me if
I were going to be here for Convocation. I said I
wasn't. He said, 'I think you should be. I think you
should change your plans.'

My heart beat faster with excitement. Was he
trying to tell me that I had got a First, or that I had
Q

won some of the prizes? It was idiotic: we were
playing with each other on the 'phone like a shy boy
and girl in their first love affair.

Then he said, 'I'm not allowed to tell you the
results. All I can say is that I'm satisfied with you, and
I haven't any doubt you will be with yourself when
the news is announced tomorrow. Obey my command, youth. Do not go to Jasper. Come out here
tomorrow and stay with us for Convocation. I will
open one of my few remaining bottles of good wine in
your honour, and Eleanor will cook us a chicken. We
will celebrate.'

I could not sleep that night, and I felt so sick the
next morning I could not go to the Notice Board to
read the results. A friend did that for me, and came
back and said 'You've swept the board'. He had
written them down on a piece of paper. I had got my
First, and the Lieutenant-Governor's Gold Medal and
the University Fellowship, and I shared the Shakespeare
prize with Harris. My immediate inclination was to
cry. The tears came to my eyes for the first time since
that day in October 1917. But it was only a momentary
impulse, the sudden relaxing of the enormous strain I
had been under. My next was to get down on my
knees and thank God, the way we used to do at home.
That impulse lasted longer. I shut the door on my
friend, and did that.

It was not much of a triumph, but almost exactly
ten years had passed since I had started out in the world
as a boy of fifteen, ignorant, oh God, how ignorant, and
lonely. When I thought of some of the dangers I had
been exposed to, and how by luck and the kindness of
friends I had managed to survive, my heart was thank-

ful, and the only way I could pour out the gratitude I was feeling was on my knees to that shadowy Presence who had brooded immense and protective over me ever since that first moment of childhood when I had stood on my own legs, not holding anyone's hand.

CHAPTER TWELVE

WHEN the autumn term opened, I found myself for the first time on the dais teaching, looking down at the faces of students instead of being amongst them and looking up at the teacher. It was a strange experience, at moments exhilarating, but frequently disheartening. At one of my first lectures the Professor came in after I had started and took an empty seat in the front row. I faltered momentarily; he waved me to go on, and I had to proceed with his eyes looking up at me. He left before the end, and afterwards made no comment.

I had to give two courses, English 1, for Freshmen, an elementary grammar and composition course; and English 53A, a Shakespeare course for third-year students, the play this year being *Romeo and Juliet*. I soon discovered that I had no vocation for teaching. There were moments of bliss when occasionally we took fire from one another, and what they felt and what I felt and what Shakespeare had meant were suddenly fused into a blinding light of understanding, and we were all enriched by it. But such moments did not come very often, and I detested the lethargy that weighed upon us all from hour to hour between such sudden illuminations. I felt that I must eventually escape, but I kept such thoughts to myself, and meanwhile worked hard at my thesis, out of which I soon began to get notions of triumphant achievement something like that felt by the crossword-puzzle addict.

This document was concerned with the pre-Shakespearean dramatist Lyly, the author of *Euphues*. He was to Shakespeare what Richardson was to Fielding or Pierce Egan to Dickens, a forerunner, infinitely less gifted, and with a much narrower view. He was a court dramatist, writing for the sophisticated audience of that confined circle, whereas Shakespeare wrote for the common man.

The only thing that made Lyly unusual was that he was at court at one of the most exciting times in a great reign. Elizabeth was being pressed to sign the death warrant of Mary Queen of Scots, and hung back from that fatal commitment, and so small was the world of the court that everyone down to the smallest groom was privy to the high drama that was in suspense.

Lyly's *Endimion* is a deadly dull play, full of the conceits that were in fashion in the court language of the time. But interwoven with the quaint action and expression is the historic debate in which all Whitehall was engaged.

Or so I thought, and so I deduced. It was plain that *Endimion* was an allegory in which the moon and the earth, like good and evil, contended for the love of England. The adulatory language made it clear that Cynthia, the moon, was Elizabeth. Endimion was Leicester. An opposing force, a contender of stature, was needed. Who could it be but Mary Queen of Scots?

It was not difficult to recreate the high drama of that moment in the history of England, and to see in Lyly's allegorical figures the chief actors of the time caught for the purposes of my argument in a *tableau vivant*. It all fitted. All that was missing was common sense. It was true that the world of the court was a small one, and that playwrights had the same licence to be familiar that court jesters in an earlier age had had. There was the coincidence that just after this play was performed Elizabeth, after long hesitation, had signed Mary's death warrant. But that she had been moved to do it by Master Lyly's play was a piece of silliness of which only an academic in pursuit of academic honours could be capable. My essay of 45 pages had been published in a learned philological journal, and having attracted some correspondence, I was invited to give a paper on the subject at a conference of English teachers at Toronto, and travelled two thousand miles each way in order to deliver this further draught of foolishness. Finally, it won me my M.A., being accepted by the university as a thesis for the degree.

I should have been very satisfied with my first essay in scholarship, but in point of fact this success had a quite unexpected effect on me. Some scales fell from my eyes. Nobody scoffed at my empty victory, nobody tried to seduce me from my aim of making a reputation in the university. But my responses were as clear and as pure as the sound of a church bell on a summer evening. I found myself ashamed of my work as a detective in pre-Shakespearean drama, and in the same flash of revelation was aware that I was proud of the humble and immature work I was doing for the *Journal*. I did not need to ask myself why. I knew that one was creative, and one was dry-as-dust academic. Foolish my creative work might be, but it was not so foolish as the puppet-play I had invented, published with all the scholarly apparatus of footnotes in a learned journal, instead of being written, delivered, set and printed in the night, and appearing on the editorial page of a provincial daily.

I kept these thoughts to myself, but the Professor was a very wise man, and knew what I was thinking, and took pleasure in shocking me by showing that he knew. 'Don't be a damn fool and fall in love with journalism,' he said. 'You are young, and like to show off. Some day you may be a creative writer, but that amusing twaddle you are writing for the *Journal* will not get you very far. A Ph.D. degree will.'

The university year was drawing to an end, and the Professor had accepted an invitation to give a course at the summer school of the University of California. In accordance with the usual custom, he was allowed to have, at the university's expense, an assistant to mark papers and take some of his classes. It was usual to pick these up locally, but the Professor decided to take me with him. We started out at the end of May in Hotspur to motor from Edmonton to Los Angeles, a distance of nearly five thousand miles. We started out in mud, for the late spring rains were falling in Alberta, and the great northern crops were but green shoots thirsting for it. We ended up two weeks later, having emerged, covered with dust, from the Mojave desert as the sun was rising, rolling along the fine road leading into Los Angeles, city of my fate, and that of how many countless others !

The summer was intensely beautiful ; air, light and sky had a clarity and power that acted in a most stimulating way on bodies and minds used to the more opaque and heavier air of northern latitudes. The

young women of this sunlit city especially, with their
bare and shapely legs, their open humour, and wide
and teasing eyes, distracted me while I attempted to per-
form my modest academic duties. I had been used to
lecturing to classes of thirty or thirty-five. Now I found
myself facing rising tiers of seats that held seven hundred.
Canadian students were garbed against the penetrating
cold; here I faced with uneasy eye what appeared to be
the inhabitants of a nudist colony who had picked up an
odd clout to keep them from going goose-fleshed while
they sat indoors. They came to lectures with tennis
racquets which they leaned against their sunburnt
legs; they came with hair wet and shining from the
pool or from some nearby ocean beach; they positively
radiated a rude and boisterous health. There was a far
higher proportion of girls to boys among the students
than there was in our northern universities. The sun
had made nearly all of them look like she-leopards,
silky and beautiful, and I felt like a newly-arrived mis-
sionary walking in the glade of an African forest while
these sleek animals lay panting in the shade, swishing
their tails in a catlike contemplative way, watching me
through sleepy eyes, as though saying to themselves
'Some time or other, when I gets the mood, Ise gwine
eat him'.

I gave one of the lectures each week on the English
novel. We started this short course with *Tom Jones*,
and we ended it with *Tess of the D'Urbervilles*.

The Professor, when he faced this Lecture Theatre,
spoke with authority; his voice thundered out the
facts, and with his wonderful powers of reading, he
could hold even this unscholarly crowd's attention. I
fancied that they could not understand what had caught

them, but they were held captive, and watched him, I noticed, with their large eyes quite curious.

But I had very little authority, and was of their own age. My carefully-prepared notes were muddled into disorder under my nervous hands as I sought to answer sensibly the questions which they aimed at me, not for elucidation of some difficult point, as I soon discovered, but to involve me in an embarrassing reply. Fielding, Richardson, Smollett and Sterne had written for a robust audience very like this one I was addressing, but my students had a lot of new-fangled psychological terms then in fashion. They wanted me to explain the sexual behaviour of Tom Jones and Roderick Random in the light of the discoveries made by Freud and Adler. This had nothing to do with literature; or had it ? At the end of our discussions I did not know; all I knew was that this was getting us nowhere in our pursuit of learning.

I do not know why many of them were there. For some it was merely a way of putting in the summer. Summer School, as it was called, provided a respectable reason for dashing off with tennis racquets and swimming shorts each morning to spend the day on the Campus in company with the opposite sex.

The University of California at Los Angeles was then situated downtown in Hollywood. It had long outgrown its limits, and was to be moved outside the city bounds to some site overlooking the ocean where a new Campus was to be laid down, and a university erected that could stand comparison with Stanford and the University of California at Berkeley in San Francisco.

The Professor and I chanced to arrive when the position of the new site was about to be announced,

and we found the regular University Faculty in a state
of frantic excitement over it. This was not because, as
might happen elsewhere in the world, there was debate
as to the attractions of alternative sites, but because a
feverish gamble was on over the land values attaching
to whatever site was eventually chosen. Everybody
was in the market at that time in the States; this was
only a year before that fatal September 1929, which
marked the arrival of Depression.

The Professor and I, entertained by permanent
members of the Faculty, were driven to inspect the
various proposed sites, and listened to the tale of the
money eventually to be made if the site finally chosen
was one into which the Faculty member entertaining us
at the moment had put his cash. It seemed an odd way
for members of the teaching profession to behave. The
Professor and I looked at each other; I saw his mouth
turn downwards at the corners, and the ash from his
cigarette was shaken off before it had time to turn grey,
so disapproving became the tremors of his old head.

Half-way through the term my seven hundred young
ones were submitted to a Test, and I marked the papers.
I could not believe that even they, these laughing
students with their minds obviously on other things,
could have done so badly. Or was it I who had taught
badly? I talked it over with the Professor, and he said,
'Don't give marks if they haven't earned them.' Well,
then, they had asked for it, and grimly I gave them their
reward. I spent the next lecture hour telling them how
badly they had done. I then asked three of the students
to distribute the papers, waited until this was done, and
then walked from the room. The whistles of dismay,
the outraged cries, the angry calls of protest were what

I had expected. What I had not expected was that some of them, and it felt like a good many of them, should pursue me down the hall to the English Faculty room. They came behind me like a swarm of bees. I shut the door, faced those of my colleagues who were there, and explained what had happened, and one of them went to the door to parley with the band. After a time they went away, leaving me in low spirits.

But I was young as well as they, and I recovered. Either they did better in the second half of the term, or I compromised a little; whatever the reason, we both emerged at the end of Summer School quite fond of each other, and with only those students scathed by failure who would have been in any case.

Just before the end of the term the President of the university invited me to dinner, and afterwards asked me if I would care to stay on and teach at the University of California instead of returning to Edmonton. The salary offered was more than half as much again as that which the University of Alberta paid me, and there was besides the powerful compulsion of the beauty and happiness I thought I found all about me in this radiant paradise. But I had at that time some grace left in me. I went to my Professor and told him of this chance, and he persuaded me that all that glitters is not gold, and made me aware, in a dear fatherly way, that some of those pleasures I loved here were superficialities, things of the flesh, not of the spirit. We made our way northward again, and the fresh, brisk air of the golden autumn drove out from the flesh the languors of that southern summer.

Then the winter snows came, and the keen bitter frost. The mercury went down, and my spirits with it.

I knew that I could not stand this work for another year, and the thought of spending two more years after that working for a Ph.D. simply appalled me. Sunk in gloom I was no fit company for anyone, and I spent long hours in the library, with open books before me to signify that I was at work and should not be disturbed. But I was engaged in daydreams of what life would be like in New York or London, if only I dared make the break, if only I could earn a living as a journalist while I found out if I really had it in me to be a writer, and could live by my pen.

New York is closer to Edmonton than London is, and it happened by an extraordinary chance that a particular god emerged from his machine to do a service for me. Just outside Edmonton a retired British Army major and his wife were living in a large house. Major Anderson was a friend of my father's, and I had been invited there several times for meals. I liked them both; they were very sophisticated and amusing, and they served wine, even sometimes champagne, at dinner, almost unheard of on the prairies at that time.

Ann Anderson was the only sister of Raoul Fleischmann, who in that very year had started the *New Yorker*. Once in that autumn term I dined alone with the Andersons, and excited by the wine, and prompted, I suppose, by the benevolent deity referred to, I confessed how much I disliked teaching, and how I longed to go to New York or London, and become a writer.

I was not laughed at. Ann and Charles Anderson said I certainly ought to try to get a job in New York or London, and she offered to write to Raoul Fleischmann on my behalf.

She was as good as her word, and in a few weeks

she showed me a letter from Raoul Fleischmann saying
that if I came to New York he would try to fit me into
a job on the *New Yorker*. There was nothing I could
do until the following May when the university year
ended, but I was greatly cheered by this chance in my
affairs, about which at this stage I said absolutely nothing
to the Professor.

Then an epidemic of chicken-pox was sent to
scourge the student-body, and the university closed two
weeks early for the Christmas vacation. I had made
many friends in Los Angeles, and had been invited by
one to come and spend the Christmas holidays with
him. I rushed off as soon as I had the grateful news of
what the epidemic had done, and twenty-four hours
later was back in the sunshine again. Though I did not
know it, I had left the snows behind me for ever.

A rich man, the vice-president of a picture company,
whom I had met during the summer term, was my host.
I was established most comfortably in a suite of immense
proportions in a corner of his house on Sunset Boulevard. He gave me a car to run round in, invited me to
do what I liked to amuse myself while he was at the
studios all day and required me only to drink with him
and discuss the soul in the evening hours. The gin was
of his own manufacture, Prohibition being still in effect
in the United States. To its ordinary qualities of taste
and power to stimulate it added the spice of danger;
embarking on an evening's drinking was like cutting
the painter and letting the boat drift on the stream; it
might float idly for a few hours and then gently nudge
the river's bank as it returned to shore, but there was
always the possibility that it might drift into a tributary
of the Styx from which there was no returning. Under

such circumstances it was not inappropriate to discuss the soul. My host, who had too easily amassed an enormous fortune with no equipment other than native cunning, felt that to muse upon God, the hereafter, and the whole divine intention, with an ice-cold Martini clutched in a warm, apprehensive palm, was the intellectual equivalent of keeping one's fingers crossed against the unwelcome return of the poverty and grimness of his youth, spent as a Jewish tailor's son in a tenement in New York.

We sat on the patio, looking out at the pale-blue evening sky. In a room somewhere behind us the gramophone would be playing dance music, and the voices of his large family formed a chattering background to the awful solemnity of our talk. I liked him; there was something massive and reliable about him which I found reassuring, and I envied him his sure instinct in dealing with the world, knowing how flaccid my own grip was upon the future. There was something wistful about him, too, and the contrast between the self-certainty of his appearance and the childlike doubt in his grey, prominent eyes, was essentially appealing.

'Gee, I wish I had your education,' he used to say, when we had pursued an argument to the limited bounds of which we were capable. 'What wouldn't I have done in the world!'

On this visit I formed another and more important attachment. I had been asked by a friend in Edmonton if I would deliver for him a Christmas present to a Mr. Frederick Hammond, who owned the Alberta Coal Company of which he was General Manager. Mr. Hammond was a man of considerable wealth and a wide range of interests who had indifferent health, and who spent part of his time in Europe and part in California, making occasional flying visits to Canada to attend to his interests there. I had heard my father speak of him with envy. The Cadomin mine, which Fred Hammond owned, was the chief rival of our mine at Brule, but our seams were worked at an irritating disadvantage compared with those of Cadomin. Ours were situated at considerable depth; shafts had to be sunk, and there was long haulage to the surface. The Cadomin seams ran near, and parallel with, the surface. As I understood it, at Cadomin you had only to make an incision in the side of the hill, and the black wealth came gushing out. Their tonnage was equal to ours, but was produced much more cheaply. The profit was enormous, and Frederick Hammond was the sole owner.

I put off my call on him until the day before Christmas, and then drove down in my borrowed car the two hundred miles to his estancia which lay between Los Angeles and San Diego. I arrived only to discover from the Manager that he had left the day before for Europe, but might be stopping over a day at the Vista del Arrayo Hotel in Pasadena. I felt concerned that I had put off delivering the present for the fortnight I had been here, and as soon as I got home telephoned the hotel. I found him there, identified myself, asked if I might come and deliver the present, received from him an assurance that I would be welcome, and drove post-haste out to Pasadena.

There were several steamer trunks already packed and labelled in the hall of one of the luxurious little cottages which the hotel let as separate establish-

ments in its garden. Hammond was about fifty, walked
with a stiff leg, supporting himself with a stick. He
had a charming and friendly manner, and was a sym-
phony in grey and blue, his suit, shirt, tie, eyes and
complexion all being one or other of these colours.
He had a soft, unaccented and most pleasant voice,
rather mesmeric in quality. His blue eyes protruded,
but had a shining, warm friendliness in their gaze that
immediately melted the icy manner which at this age I
always exposed at first contact with anyone rich or
famous, or more wise than I claimed myself to be.

We spoke of our competing coal mines, and I told
him of my university life and career; what I was doing
in California, and with whom I was staying.

'A poor life for an energetic man, this teaching,' he
said. 'You work only half the year.'

He had read my articles and regularly read my
column in the *Journal*, which he had sent to him
wherever he was in the world. I must have blushed
with pride at this recognition of my published works,
for he laughed and said,

'Makes you feel good, doesn't it, to have been read
in New York, Paris, London and Monte Carlo? See
how much further one written word travels than all
your eloquence in your English lectures at the university.'

I longed to ask him what advice he could give me
about writing in earnest, and for a larger public. I was
perfectly content to go on talking about my own
affairs, but he suddenly made signs of distress, putting
his hands up to his throat as though he were choking;
and while I watched him, rather alarmed, he drew
himself up stiffly from his chair, walked a pace or two
to the mantelpiece and pressed a bell.

In a moment a nurse appeared. She put her arm about him, and they went from the room, he leaning heavily on her and his stick. I was left alone, not knowing whether I should depart or wait to be dismissed. Minutes passed, and then the nurse returned.

'I'm afraid Mr. Hammond is not well enough to say goodbye to you, and as we leave for New York at six o'clock tonight he must rest. He asks me to say how sorry he is.'

I had never had an interview that had ended like that one, starting so warmly and ending so abruptly. He was nice, I thought, as I walked to the car. I wished I had known him better. For I felt, even after this brief meeting, stimulated in mind and ambition, and I determined there and then that in the fortnight I had left to spend in California I would make a start on a book I had been dreaming of writing for the past three years.

I had no sooner got back to the house, hung up my hat and walked out to the patio than I was summoned to the telephone.

'Hammond here,' said the voice; it sounded frail and ill. 'So sorry we had to break off our conversation like that. Look here, can you come back at four o'clock this afternoon? I should like to speak to you about something. You can? Good man. Until four o'clock, then.'

I heard the click of the disconnection before I had replaced the receiver. But I was in a trance for only a moment; the next, a sense of enormous excitement was welling up in me. 'Don't be a fool,' I admonished

R

myself as I went back to the patio. 'Because he briefly
mentioned your articles, and, don't forget, almost immediately felt sick, you think he wants to pursue that
subject. Most likely he wants you to take something
back to Edmonton for him.' But admonish this hope
as I would, it persisted until I found myself in his
sitting-room again that afternoon; and then it died.
Something of the warmth and friendliness of his manner
in the morning had gone; he was not unfriendly, but
he was businesslike and abrupt, as though he had a duty
to get over. The sooner he did it, the sooner he would
be free of it and of me.

'When do you go back to Edmonton ?' he asked.

'In ten days.'

He made no response to this, looking not at me
but down at his watch-chain which he slipped up
and down through his fingers. The silence was marked
and uncomfortable for what should have been merely
a social call, but I could not think how to break it. He
broke it himself, looking up suddenly, and speaking
quickly.

'I said this morning that you were wasting your
time teaching. You are, you know. You might
amount to something in serious journalism if you had
a chance. I've decided to give you that chance, provided you'll take it right away.'

He looked down again, and I remember that he was
silent for a moment or two, and the excitement I felt
was as agonizing as sharp physical pain. He looked up
at last and went on.

'I've just bought the *English Review*. Do you know
it ? I am going over to England now to take it over.
I'll take you on as my assistant, helping me to plan the

organization, and when I take over the *Review* I'll make you assistant editor.   Would you like that ?'

Like it ! I wrung my clasped hands and yearned at him.

'You could leave tonight, or say in three or four days' time ?   I'm sailing on the *Mauretania* on the 31st. I should want you to go with me.'

The face of the Professor rose up in my thoughts, cold and reproving as it had been during some of my early interviews with him.   There was no chance of the university finding someone to take my place for the rest of the year at such short notice.   Lecturers in English, though little value was evidently attached to them by the rest of the world, were not there to be picked up at any moment on the streets of prairie cities. The Professor would not let me go, unless, using his liking for me, I could persuade him to accept inconvenience for himself in order to help me to this wonderful opportunity, for that I was convinced it was.

I tried to persuade Frederick Hammond to hold the job open for me until May, but he was insistent that I should come right away or not at all.   After a useless and silent struggle with my conscience, I agreed, and promised that I would join him in New York, if the university would let me go, on the 31st.   Instantaneously with that, he dropped his brisk, businesslike manner, became warm and friendly again, insisted that I should share with him a bottle of champagne to drink our respective healths and that of our magazine; then, when the car was announced at the door ready to take him to the station, we shook hands and parted until our meeting in New York on the 31st.

I drove home, elated by what had happened, and no doubt by the champagne, too.   It did not strike me as

R 2

odd that an employer should crack a bottle of champagne with a newly-acquired employee. I took this as an indication of the estimation in which he held my journalistic abilities, displayed so far, I omitted to remind myself, in a mining camp weekly and in a column of pedestrian quality in a daily paper with a circulation of about 25,000. I was a green and callow boy, and I am amazed now to think that Fate could tolerate such youthful arrogance.

I drove downtown and carefully composed a long night-telegram to the Professor, begging that he would accept my immediate resignation so that I could seize this wonderful opportunity. The answer came back next afternoon. It was brief and angry: 'Quite impossible to accept your suggestion. Return at once.' I was bitterly disappointed at that, and angry at the same time that he should command me to return so peremptorily. But I sent another night-telegram, urging in even more passionate terms that I should be allowed to go with good grace; I added that I wanted his blessing more than anything, but if I could not have it I would have to go anyhow. And then silence fell, and continued during the 27th and 28th until I was near the point of desperation, and at last, early on the morning of the 29th, the answer came. In my mind's ear I could hear the slamming of a door in my life. The telegram read: 'President accepts your resignation effective December 31st. Farewell.'

But though my heart should have been touched by the Professor's generosity to me, or moved and I think

it was, by the solemn finality of his message, it was
much more agitated by something else. I could not now
reach New York by the 31st. Would Hammond hold
the job for me if I came over on the boat following his ?

I wired him to New York to say that the university
had only just accepted my resignation, that it was impossible to reach him by the 31st and would he cable
me instructions as to what I was to do. Then followed
ten of the most agonizing days in my life. No reply
came from Hammond. Day after day passed. I sent
a second and a third telegram, but no answer came.
The idiot I had been to throw up a safe university post
for a foolish will-o'-the-wisp of this kind was revealed
to me in stark simplicity. I saw myself an outcast
from the academic world, incapable of earning a living
at anything else, prevented by a temporary entry permit
from working in the United States, and without enough
money to go elsewhere in the Empire and find something else. I kicked myself for a fool, and felt so sick
with despair, that between despising myself and feeling
sorry for myself I was kept feebly but unhappily
occupied.

Then on the tenth day a telegram came, and in a
moment all grief was banished. It read : 'Sorry unable
reply before to your telegram. So glad you have been
released. Wiring you one thousand dollars. Meet me
Hôtel de Paris Monte Carlo in three weeks.'

There was an unnecessary magnificence of gesture
in this which should have increased my misgivings.
Young men of twenty-five do not mistrust their powers ;

they have a lover's faith in the good turns that luck can do for them, but there were circumstances here which should have aroused the suspicions of anyone with a normal amount of caution in his character. The money Hammond had wired me was more than double what I needed to get to Monte Carlo. And why, for God's sake, Monte Carlo ! The *English Review* was in London. He had told me he was going there to take it over. Had he, with that unpredictability of behaviour that rich men are alone allowed to practise, changed his plans ? Had I ruined my whole career by an ill-considered move by which at one blow I had lost the Professor's friendship and my livelihood, and was I now being offered a holiday in romantic Monte Carlo as a consolation ?

I confess that all these horrid possibilities presented themselves to me, and for a moment I did them the honour of looking at a prospect I had not had to face since 1920, that of being without a job. But only for a moment. I was swept on by hope. My friends in Los Angeles, especially the ones at the university, who had been forced to share every moment of my suspense and agony in the last ten days, urged me to wire Hammond at Monte Carlo asking for a service agreement, or a contract of employment of some sort, before rushing off at the bidding of a telegram, which had not even been followed up by a letter. But I did not need a 'contract of employment' to assure me that my future was waiting for me with a benign smile.

I arrived in Monte Carlo to the day three weeks later. I could have arrived two days earlier, but I was so anxious to give evidence of my ability to carry out instructions to the letter that I waited over in Paris. I had never been there before, but my father had told me of his visits, and it had been the background of so much that I had read. Paris is unique among the cities of the world, and I suppose that each man has his own view of it. To me it was the city of love, where every man had his mistress and every woman her lover. The atmosphere to me was charged with passionate intrigue; and when a girl came near me, if it was only to wait on me at a restaurant table or to make up my room in the hotel, I felt something that was almost like an electric shock, and then a loss of breath and a thudding of the heart that were quite painful. I suppose that I had read too much, and knew too little, about life.

And if Paris had that effect, imagine the impression that Monte Carlo made. It had been raining on the evening we left Paris, and in my imagination, when it was not absorbed with visions, some of them a little apprehensive, of the last stage of my journey, the lovers of Paris had merely lost a little in social standing, but lost nothing of their ardour; it was a night for middle-class coal fires, crocheted curtains, red-plush eiderdowns, and plump grocers and young girls, rather than dark, tired men and mysterious women. To go to sleep in the rain and wake up in the sunshine, to leave stone buildings dark and glistening in the wet and arrive in Monte Carlo, and hear the murmur of the tideless sea, smell the flowers, see in the gloaming, as I walked up the steps which led from the station to the hotel, the lights gleaming in the gardens, and to feel the soft air on my face: this was an hour in my life that is in memory like a platform bathed in golden light to which a long tunnel leads up, and from which another has led away.

Anything was possible in this magical atmosphere.
I could have taken on any job; I felt power running
into me, and intelligence alive and quivering in me,
longing to match itself with some enterprise, the stiffer
the better. I was hungry for work, but I was to be kept
waiting.

Hammond greeted me affably in the sitting-room
of his suite, and said I must be tired after my journey.
He had reserved a room for me in the hotel, and he
would see me the next day at noon. I was dismissed.
I walked down the wide hall. Somehow I was disappointed, and I could not tell why. I could hardly have
expected him to put me to work that very night, but I
knew that something very important had been left out
of our short conversation. He had not said why we
were here instead of in London. He had not mentioned
the name that was burned into my brain as that of Calais
was in the heart of Queen Mary; he had said nothing
about the *English Review*.

O God, what singleness of purpose does for one!
On that lovely night in January I wandered unhappily
to the steps of the Hôtel de Paris and gazed with an
anxious heart at the lights in the gardens below. I was
in love with an idea. It would have been better, I see
now, to have been in love with a girl. But the idea
devoured me, and I suffered on its account just as many
pangs as young lovers do who are uncertain still of their
happiness; she could hide her face from me, she could
seem to disappear, to grow cold and devote herself
to another, and then with a divine smile of surrender
appear to be almost within reach; and withdraw just
as I was about to seize her.

So the flowers, the scented sea, the riches and the

beauty everywhere at which I was looking for the first time in my life were wasted on me, and I turned and went to my room and stared at my luggage. But I could not bear to unpack it. That would mean accepting a supposition which I had resolutely refused to accept when I had been in Los Angeles, that Hammond had changed his mind. If he had, I would go on myself. I could not buy magazines; in fact, come to think of it, I did not even have enough to pay my railway fare to London. But somehow or other I would get there. I had not come so far now only to turn back. I stuck my clenched fists in my pockets and walked up and down my room, catching sight at each turn of my bags, my unbeautiful companions which had followed me like a pair of faithful Sancho Panzas ever since the madness had seized me, as it did Don Quixote, to leave his home and broaden his operations.

When we met at noon the sun was shining brilliantly. Hammond looked frail and ill, but he greeted me with a warm and friendly smile, and suggested that we stroll over and sit in the sunshine outside the Café de Paris. His nurse wrapped him up in thick mufflers and he wore a heavy overcoat. He walked with a pronounced limp, very slowly and evidently with a good deal of pain. We dragged our way across the Square, and I looked at the man whose trail I was following in this romantic and uncertain fashion half across the world. I was by now definitely uneasy. He looked very far indeed from well. It was difficult to imagine that he could even deal with the negotiations to purchase the magazine, let alone run it afterwards.

He told me that he had developed pneumonia just as he was about to sail on the *Mauretania*, and had been taken from his hotel to a hospital. That explained why he had not written immediately in reply to my telegram. He was very glad I had been able to come and join him. The plans for taking over the *English Review* had been delayed for a month or so because the owner, Mr. Ernest Remnant, had gone to Russia as leader of the British Industrial Mission, and would not be back until early March. Meanwhile, he told me, I was not to worry. He had paid a deposit of £1000 against the purchase price of £10,000. The delay would be good for us both. It would enable him to convalesce fully from his illness, and he and I could work together on plans for revitalizing the *English Review* and making it once again into the great journal it had been before the first World War.

All this was comforting for me to hear, and should have been reassuring. But there were some things about it that I did not like. Hammond's state of health was one. If he collapsed, so would our plans. I did not like the idea of lazing about in the South of France for a month or more; it seemed to me a much better idea that I should go on to London, and if possible work in the *English Review* office as his representative, so that we might be ready to take over without interruption. This was the third thing that made me uneasy. When I made this quite sensible suggestion, his underlip trembled like a baby's and his blue eyes clouded over with disappointment. He had a most expressive face and could hide nothing. 'No, I don't think so,' he said. 'It is also important that I should get to know you.'

★

So we settled down into what became for me an almost intolerable existence. I lived in a splendid room in the Hôtel de Paris, the windows of which opened on to the Casino Square and to the blue sea beyond. I rose about eleven, for a reason which will be apparent in a moment. For an hour I worked at plans for the *Review*. At twelve, we went to the garden outside the Café de Paris, drank cocktails and sat in the sun. At one we lunched in the Café. A siesta until three, and then either a game of golf at Mont Agel or a motor drive. From six to eight a little more work; then dinner either at the Café or the casino. At eleven we went to the tables and played there until two o'clock. Then back to the hotel, a bottle of champagne and chicken sandwiches, and long talk, myself stupid with sleep, until 5 or 6 A.M., when I would be allowed to go to bed. It was not surprising that I did not rise until eleven. When I did get up I felt pale, unsteady and unhappy. It might have been romantic, this life; but it was depressing to the digestion and dismaying to ambition.

All that was stern and Scottish in my character and breeding rebelled against the softness and repellent luxury of this unnatural existence. And all that was proud and self-assertive rebelled, too, against duties and obeisances from which all my life I had been free. For all his kindness and generosity to me, for all his intelligence and likeability, this man as I got to know him better, asked too much in return. He was rich and had an inborn petulance of spirit, and an unexpressed grudge against life for the few small injuries it had done him. And what were these, when he named them ? A stiff leg, and lack of appreciation by the world of the artistic-creative genius he felt he possessed, but had never been able freely to employ because of the time consumed by the commercial enterprises from which he derived his wealth. He could not shrug this failure off, and I think his stiff leg was a hypochondriacal gesture of the injury he suspected himself to have received; the slow halting step was visible evidence of why he had not been able to keep up with other men in the race.

The unconventional hours we kept, though not inappropriate to Monte Carlo, were dictated by the fact that he suffered from insomnia. Perforce I suffered, too, though I was all for yielding to sleep, and underwent agonies submitting to insomnia instead. He believed that sleep could be induced if face towels, soaked in cold water, were wrung out and then wrapped around his bare feet. In the dawn hours, in our shuttered rooms, the air of which was heavy and stale with the scent of his Turkish cigarettes, I would move wearily from the bathroom to his bedroom, engaged in this revolting task, and in between sit nodding in a chair by his bed while he delivered long soliloquies on life and death and sex and art.

I nodded, but did not sleep. It came to me slowly, with a growing sense of shock and fright, that I had got myself into a terrible predicament, and that unless I extricated myself quickly, my future was as much ruined as though I had never made the physical and mental effort I had done in these last few years.

I saw myself becoming a nurse to this self-indulgent man, becoming, in fact, a body-servant with no dignity and no hope. Bitterly I regretted having given up my old job, and once, in the very pit of depression, I wrote to the Professor asking if I could have my post back again. I deserved the curt answer he sent. I had left of my own accord, my place had been filled, and there was no possibility, nor ever would be, that the university would require my services again.

That flick of the whip was what I needed. I knew now that I was out on my own, and after a moment with my heart in my mouth, I swallowed that, and a feeling of exhilaration swept over me, tumbling me joyfully as a surf-wave does a swimmer walking out to meet it. The swimmer responds instinctively, and so did I. I was on my own, as I had so often been in the years before I went to university. But now I was almost within reach of the literary world I had so longed to enter; one more stroke, one powerful thrust, and I would be there.

An interesting contrast existed between the elderly man lying in his rich dressing-gown on his canopied bed, dreaming aloud and rather fearfully of what he meant to do with the *English Review* when he got hold of it, and the sharp-featured young man with the tired eyes, leaning forward in his chair and dreaming his contrapuntal part of what he might do with this great journal when Hammond had tired of it, as a rich man would, and had gone back to Canada, or south, after the sun. How the fates, in whose hands are the threads of our destinies must have smiled to observe the scene! Or perhaps glanced in sharp wonder at how near to getting what he ardently desires the really determined human being can come.

January passed into February. Ernest Remnant remained in Russia on his Industrial mission, and we looked like spending the rest of the winter on the

Riviera. We moved from Monte Carlo to Cannes, and joined up at the Hôtel de Provence with Mrs. Hammond and her five beautiful daughters, newly arrived from Canada. These brought me, with their beauty, youth and high spirits, a relaxation of the intolerable strain I had been under in Monte Carlo, but hope deferred maketh the heart sick, and I still languished and longed for the summons to come from London, even when I was playing tennis with these charming girls, or dancing with them in the evening.

Those months, spent in more luxurious surroundings than any I have known since, were the most troubled in my life, comparable in the depression of spirit they engendered with those which had followed my mother's death. In the ten years that had passed since those lonely winter nights in Ottawa, I had slowly learnt to single out from all that life offers when one is young and energetic and full of hope, the reward that I aimed for : it was to write. Not to teach, not necessarily to be a creative writer, not to write only as a writer who wrests a living from his pen : but to be concerned with writing, to make words, which I loved, which had been my support and my companions through all these difficult years, the means of my livelihood as well as of my constant pleasure.

It did not strike me as unusual that one who but a few years before had been Editor of the *Blue Diamond Weekly* in a Rocky Mountain mining town, should be fussing now because of the delay in his appointment as Assistant Editor of the *English Review* in London. It seemed to me maddening that I should have come ninety-nine/one hundredths of the way, and be held up at the last moment by this delay ; two wealthy men, one in Russia, and one in Monte Carlo, between them preventing me from grappling with my fate. Eating rich food, and drinking wine to which I was not accustomed, no doubt deepened my melancholy and gave me too much time for brooding.

I thought I had discovered something about Frederick Hammond. He was afraid. He had that most haunting of all forms of fear, the fear of fracturing the bright consoling image he clutched of himself, the image of a clever man who but for the accidents of fate would have succeeded. That dragging leg dragged more, those fainting fits overpowered him when he was forced to make a decision which might not turn out to be a wise one.

Engaging me as an editorial assistant had given him a bad turn; the purchase of the *English Review*, which in his dreams he saw himself as editing, becoming what he had longed to become — a literary figure in London, far away from that rich mountain of coal in Alberta — had given him another and more prolonged attack of nerves. I could see now that he regretted having taken me on and brought me all this way. At the same time he did not want to lose me, for he knew that eventually he would have to face the conclusion of this deal.

Suddenly, one morning, there was a letter from Hammond's solicitors in London to say that Remnant had returned from Russia, and was asking whether we meant to proceed with the deal, or was the £1000 deposit to be regarded as forfeit.

This produced an agonizing collapse, but it gave me my opportunity. I urged him to let me go ahead to London, and look into details of the purchase, and suggested that he should follow me as soon as he was well enough. He agreed, and my departure was fixed for three or four days afterwards. The hour of my deliverance was at hand; of his, too. It must be a relief to be rid of a gadfly.

The white cliffs of England leaned back proudly from the green sea, and the gulls wheeled and dipped about us with their disapproving outraged cries. The smell of salt water was sharp and pungent. The tugs and little freighters dashed past and cut across our bows, streaming black smoke from their dirty funnels, and glistening waves from their bows. There was intense movement everywhere; the wind was sharp and fresh. I was a passenger in the Channel packet, sailing into Dover Harbour, and I could hardly credit it. I had joined a pathway which had been followed by some of the greatest literary figures of the past. Byron and Shelley had come this way, Wordsworth returning from Belgium, the Brownings coming back from Italy, Dickens returning from France, and countless others. All approaching London, the literary workshop of the English world, as I was now, with their manuscripts and ideas, with lines singing in their heads, with plans for books yet unwritten. They had stood against the rail watching, as I did, the white cliffs of England rising up from the sea. I felt ecstatically happy. My mind, busy with its dreams, kept returning to the past, as though I must continually remind myself how extraordinarily lucky, how favoured by the fates, I had been.

It seemed years since I had left the university, huddled against the white earth high on the wind-swept escarpment above the Saskatchewan River. I would never be able to look back on that lost world without a feeling of regret for the way in which I had left it. I could not shake from my mind an image of the Professor with cold indifferent look fixed sternly on me, where once his gaze had been warm and interested and involved in my affairs. I looked back along the road I had come, and in truth it seemed lined with the casualties of my friends and those who had loved me, from Mac in Maisonneuve to the Professor in Edmonton. Every one of them had done something to my life, and I had touched them as I had moved to this point of entry where I now paused, filled with the wildest hopes. It was sad to realize that I had no friends, that no one now remained who loved me for my own sake, or for whose sake I would turn aside from my goal. I had given my capacity for love, along with everything else, to the thing which had never failed me, the power and beauty of words, the moving, wonderful thoughts they can embody, the sweet comfort of words.

In a moment of clarity about myself I saw the mistake I was making: People are more important than words; happiness is more satisfying than success. But the subtle drug had been an addiction too long for me to pretend that I could master it. When had it begun to fasten on me? Perhaps in those early days in Australia when my father read me books too exciting for a young mind to bear. I should have been fed on the pap prepared for children.

Perhaps in Africa, when I found I could enslave Harry with my own version of the word? No, it was in those lonely months following my mother's death, when words were my only friends, the constant friends, I had. I could still remember those lonely, unhappy nights with horror. But how much more horrible they would have been if I had had to sit staring at a wall, and had not been able to lose myself in a world created by others, or in the ones I tried to create for myself.

The Professor had rescued me from oblivion, and sent me on. It was no good his looking wounded, and useless for me to have a conscience about him. The moment for which all my life had been a preparation was at hand.

I was far from sure of myself, but I was not a bit afraid. I knew that there was a lot of trouble still ahead, but I was spoiling for the fight; and the cold wind blowing from the Channel, the white cliffs leaning back, the choppy harbour water slapping against the quay as I walked down the gangplank, seemed to me not strange, but the setting I had expected for my entry.

I looked at the English faces and could have smiled with fond love of them, they were so familiar, so expected, so much a part of the England we all knew from Shakespeare and Dickens, and everyone who has written about the English character. Porters were bustling down from the ship loaded with bags, stewards and railwaymen passed about between the ship and the customs shed. I listened to their voices, and could have laughed for pleasure, knowing, whatever lay ahead, that I had left the ante-room where the first twenty-five years of my life had been spent and had pushed open, and closed firmly behind me, a door that led into a larger room.

THE END